GY... /POINTS

Once Upon a Gypsy Moon

Once Upon a Gypsy Moon

A Memoir

*An Improbable Voyage and One Man's
Yearning for Redemption*

Michael Hurley

**CENTER
STREET**

New York Boston Nashville

Center Street
Hachette Book Group
237 Park Avenue
New York, NY 10017

CenterStreet.com

Printed in the United States of America

RRD-C

First Edition: April 2013
10 9 8 7 6 5 4 3 2 1

Center Street is a division of Hachette Book Group, Inc.
The Center Street name and logo are trademarks of Hachette Book Group, Inc.

The Hachette Speakers Bureau provides a wide range of authors for speaking events. To
find out more, go to www.HachetteSpeakersBureau.com or call (866) 376-6591.

The publisher is not responsible for websites (or their content) that are not owned by the
publisher.

Library of Congress Cataloging-in-Publication Data
Hurley, Michael C.
  Once upon a Gypsy Moon : an improbable voyage and one man's yearning for
redemption / Michael Hurley. -- First edition.
      pages cm
  Summary: "Michael Hurley, an experienced attorney and former professional sailor,
returns to the sea to give us a thought-provoking memoir of a man's yearning for
redemption and renewal in the wake of infidelity, divorce, and failure" --Provided by the
publisher
  ISBN 978-1-4555-2933-9 (hardcover) -- ISBN 978-1-4555-2934-6 (ebook)
1. Hurley, Michael C. 2. Hurley, Michael C.--Travel. 3. Sailing. 4. Ocean travel. 5.
Seafaring life. 6. Divorce--Psychological aspects--Case studies. 7. Failure
(Psychology)--Case studies. 8. Redemption--Case studies. 9. Sailors--United
States--Biography. 10. Lawyers--United States--Biography. I. Title.
  G540.H825 2013
  910.4092--dc23
  [B]   2012041841

Contents

Contents

Contents

Preface

The story you are about to read follows the contours of a dream that I share with thousands of others: to sail a small boat over the open ocean, bound for no destination but the horizon. That dream began to unfold in August 2009 at a particularly dark time in my life. Reeling from personal failure, a bruising divorce, and the loss of a job, I found solace in the biblical commission to "put out into the deep" and left Annapolis to begin a thousand-mile, single-handed passage to Nassau. Sailing an aging but able thirty-two-foot sloop, the *Gypsy Moon*, I was not hoping to save others. I was the one who was lost. I needed to regain my bearings and find a new sense of purpose for my life.

It gives away nothing of the story to tell you that on my voyage, I failed miserably and succeeded in ways I never could have imagined. In this memoir, I have recorded observations and discoveries from the inward and the outward journey, and I have attempted to chart a course for others who may find themselves looking to begin again from a similar place in their lives. For the sailor, I have written a sea story that I hope will prove to be worth its salt. For the romantic,

Preface

I have retold a fairy tale about two lovers who found each other as well as the courage to answer Mark Twain's call to "sail away from the safe harbor" together.

It may be important to understand that most of this book was adapted from six letters that I published for a small group of long-time readers, friends, and family between November 2010 and November 2011. In putting together the book, I made some changes in the wording and organization of these letters, but overall, the narrative is the same. The last chapter, which records events that occurred well after the sixth and final letter was written, was not part of the original manuscript for the book. In hindsight, however, I don't think the story would have made sense without it. Thus are we reminded that books really write themselves; the author is just the medium.

Here you will discover many of the joys and some of the sorrows of my life as well as my innermost hopes and dreams. I hope that in this discovery you feel you have found a friend. Perhaps someday we will meet to share other stories of the sea, life, and love. Until then, I wish you fair winds.

LATITUDE 38.97.86 N

LONGITUDE 76.47.61 W

ANNAPOLIS, MARYLAND

Chapter 1

TO SAIL

In this day and age, which is to say a time well removed from the Age of Exploration, an era when there is less urgent need for travel and more efficient means to do so when one must, it would seem at the very least a mistake of judgment to point the bow of a small sailing vessel seaward and let slip her lines. One could offer clinical evidence that it is indeed an act of insanity, but that would risk missing the poetry of such a thing. Poetry or not, it is an odd habit, peering over the rail of a seagoing ship in a fifteen-knot breeze. Alone. And late in the day.

I know this pathology and have wrestled with this same impulse many times, usually regaining my heading and my senses and returning to port. Sailing alone or in company offshore, all night in a small boat, is a thing that passes for mere eccentricity or even dashing adventure in polite company. But however benign, it remains nonetheless a disorder, a departure from the mean and median of human life, and a path that many regard with admiration or envy but that few decide to follow. There are, I am told, more men alive today who have flown in outer space than who have sailed alone

3

around the world by no power save what wind and water might supply. I am not surprised by this, nor would you be if you sailed with me.

What appeals to me about voyaging in a small boat under sail is what first appealed to me as a young boy about camping in the wilderness. Both are simple systems—or, more accurately, systems for achieving simplicity. Aboard a boat, life is reduced to its essential elements. Life as we live it in the modern world, by contrast, has become a very complicated thing. We take the first steps toward school, career, and marriage, and before we know it, we are swept up into a self-perpetuating cyclone of consumption and production, to be carried aloft on those busy winds until we are thrown back to Earth some seventy-five years later, wondering where all the time and money have gone. We consume, and so we produce; we produce, and so we consume.

In a boat at sea, the processes of consumption and production are conjoined. That's the beauty of it. The wind and water are at once both spectacle and vehicle, means and medium. The steady breeze on our face enthralls us as it propels us. The sea bears us up and feeds us dinner. There is no Walmart there. There is nothing to buy. There is only to be.

In the city of Miami, the sky burns with electric light and the streets boil with the perpetual motion of cars and trucks and people, but just three miles off that coast, there is no traffic, no noise, and no light at night save the moon and the stars. The open ocean is the only place on Earth where the hand of man has taken no lasting hold.

I don't know what compelled me to follow the seaward path again, that August day in Annapolis. Perhaps it was a desire to retake the helm of my own destiny, however briefly. I must say I felt in that moment no small affinity with the author of the autobiography

Papillon, played by Steve McQueen in the film, who upon leaping into the sea and climbing onto a floating raft of coconuts—finally escaping Devil's Island in his old age—yells to unseen listeners, "I'm still here, you bastards."

I wish to take a moment to reassure any readers who, perhaps not familiar with me and my station in life, may be laboring under the mistaken impression that sailing is nothing but an idle pastime of the very rich. It is that in some circles, to be sure, but in general that sort of sailor loves racing, not cruising. He goes screaming about the bay with a gang of like-minded friends, ties up his expensive boat at the yacht club pier at the end of the day, savors his victory or plots his revenge in the yacht club bar, and drives back to his expensive home to await the next contest. For this man, sailing is a sport, not a frame of mind or a philosophy of life. It is, to him, very much like a game of golf played on the water. In stark contrast to this fellow, there is an entirely different breed of peasant sailors who are not more than sea gypsies, and while I cannot claim truly to be one of them, I have admired them from afar.

In fact, the rich and powerful make up the decided minority of the sailors I meet at sea. Many manage to stay just a boat length or two ahead of their bankers' worst fears, and all their fragile dreams depend heavily on the continued beneficence of a favorable wind, a half inch of duct tape, and the Dow Jones Industrial Average—hardly bulwarks of constancy. Whereas it has been famously written that the rich are different from you and me, real sailors are very different from the rich. They are an addicted bunch (insufferable cheapskates, the lot of them), and not for nothing are they regarded contemptuously in posh marinas the world around as "ragbaggers." You are likely to find more impressive balance sheets at the tailgate party of any college football game—that seemingly most egalitarian of pastimes—than among the skinned-knuckled old men in well-stained khakis and sockless Top-Siders, eyeing pots of varnish at your local ship chandlery.

I am not speaking of "yachtsmen" here—those well-fed denizens of resort marinas, marking time from one gin and tonic to the next along the inland waterways, who dream mostly of time-shares in Miami, not of Magellan, and whose dreams are born aloft by diesel fumes, not wind and imagination. Nor am I speaking of those who rent sailboats on Caribbean vacations and (mostly) motor them nervously from one anchorage to the next.

To me, sailing is a way of looking at life, or it is nothing. It is a philosophy, not a space on one's calendar between the Friday board meeting and Sunday brunch. The kind of adventure of which I speak cannot be rented any more than true love can be rented, nor is it merely an "experience" to be had, like a game of bowling or a good cigar. Voyaging under sail is a marriage of man and vessel, and as in any healthy marriage, the bond grows stronger even as the excitement of new love mellows. The things that strengthen that bond are the patience to endure and the commitment to overcome hardship. Patience and commitment are the heart of a sailor. In life, in love, and in boats, you're either all in or you're out.

This book is partly an effort to work out the navigational problems of the heart—to find true north; to account for set, drift, variation, and deviation and measure the time and distance run, that I might better know my position within what Tolkien called "some larger way," and that others might better find the lights to guide their own voyages. Every ocean voyage forges both inward and seaward. The challenges of the seaward course that can be met are met easily enough by simple implements and routines of planning and preparation. The inward journey is not so well charted, and "there be dragons" along that way. So, with these thoughts in mind, let us cast off.

Chapter 2

A Voyage Begins

I stepped off a plane at Baltimore-Washington International Airport in August 2009 and made my way to the traffic of cars picking up passengers on the street below. It was an easy flight from Raleigh. I carried no luggage save what fit in a small duffel held with one hand. Walking into the bright morning sun, I felt the still, moist heat that, for a period however brief every summer, makes Maryland seem like Miami.

My boat, a thirty-two-foot sloop named the *Gypsy Moon*, lay just outside Annapolis in a shipyard on the Magothy River, where I had taken her for major repairs six months before. The strain of thirty seasons of sailing since she first slipped her builder's traces had taken its toll, and the work necessary to fit her out for an ocean voyage had taken five months to complete. I had undergone some less visible but no less critical repairs myself in the past few years. Now the *Gypsy Moon* was ready, and so was I.

My sister and her husband met me at the airport to ferry me to the boat, but not before the obligatory lunch of Maryland crab cakes and farewells to my brother and his family, who live nearby. In the past year and a half, while the boat was berthed in Annapolis, I had relished weekends sailing around the bay in places where, growing up, I had only imagined I might one day stand at the helm of my own boat. Here, in my middle age, I had sailed the *Gypsy Moon* under the shadow of the statehouse that was America's Revolutionary War capitol and the place where my service as a legislative intern, at age eighteen, had convinced me never to enter politics. Back in these old haunts, I had fun reconnecting with family and friends and imagining the life I might have had here if I had chosen differently between job offers in two cities—one in Houston, one in Baltimore—twenty-five years ago.

But before long, my plans to prove Thomas Wolfe wrong about going home again ran into reality. A sojourn of three decades in Texas and North Carolina had made me more accustomed to the civility of southern manners and less tolerant of the edgy combativeness of life up north. It's not just that the drivers won't let you in on the road up there. I recall passing abeam of another boat on the bay near Baltimore and leaning over the rail with a smile, ready to exchange what in southern waters would surely have been a friendly hello, and being startled by a broadside of profanity instead. (I had dared to come close.) Dumbfounded, I could manage no reaction but to say "I'm terribly sorry" and tack. It seemed that a good share of the population between Washington and Baltimore had grown accustomed to living with their dukes up. I decided that there is more to the warmth down south than the weather. I was eager to be off again, aboard the *Gypsy Moon*.

Over lunch, I answered questions from my family that gently probed the perimeters of my plans. Nassau seemed far away and nigh unattainable, not just to them, but to me as well. It's not every day, after all, that one ships out to sea alone. It sounded more daring than it was, yet I not only understood but shared their concerns. The open ocean is no trifling thing, even on the best of days.

I feel right at home at the helm of a sailboat, although I didn't come by that knowledge easily. Growing up in Maryland, I was the youngest child by ten years of a divorced mother of four, spoiled rotten by my two older sisters, too young to know my brother when he was growing up, and all but abandoned at the age of two by an alcoholic father whose absence was most acutely felt in a boy's unfulfilled dreams of grand adventure. The world of seafaring was the stuff of Hollywood—unimaginable, and far from me. As a child I lived my dreams on a much smaller scale, on creeks and ponds that I could reach on foot, in nearby neighborhoods, and on scouting trips with the aid of the fathers of other boys. It was mostly about the fishing back then, and the smell of wood smoke, and the authenticity of living life in the rough—however briefly, and never far from the ready-to-eat suburban comforts of 1960s America. Those truant days in the woods were wonderful furloughs, allowing my imagination to inhabit a world apart from teachers and tests. I loved the unsupervised freedom of it all.

But Chesapeake Bay and the sea that lay beyond were distant and more impenetrable mysteries, brought closer to me only occasionally when my brother, Jay, would take me and my sisters out for day sails aboard various dories and dinghies—some he rented, some he purchased, and one he had built himself. I distinctly recall the moment when the bow of a Rhodes 19 sloop, with my brother at the helm, plunged out of the mouth of the South River into the chop of the broader waters of Chesapeake Bay. What was once a horizon of trees and houses became nothing but water and the unseen possibility of whatever lay beyond. I looked into the small space of the cuddy cabin beneath the mast, just big enough for a duffel of food and clothes, and wondered what it might be like if we just *kept going*.

We didn't. When our hour was up we pointed that fearless ship of dreams sheepishly homeward, paid for the time used, and drove back to the city on dry land. But the infection of that moment and others like it remained with me and would reemerge often years later, beginning with the time when I decided to "borrow" Jay's fourteen-foot sloop and take her sailing myself.

Chapter 3

WEATHER SIGNS

It was 1976. I was eighteen, and my brother was away on his honeymoon. "Borrowing" Jay's boat for a day of sailing seemed the perfect way to impress a girl on a first date, but my plans ended abruptly when a gust of wind reached the mainsail more quickly than my hand reached the mainsheet. In an instant, all that once had been proud and skyward was scandalized and submerged. The girl swam ashore. Perched like an indignant wet bird on top of the floating, overturned hull, I stoically waited for the coast guard to arrive. They eventually came and, with more horsepower than horse sense, dragged the capsized sloop to shallow water without righting her first, and snapped off the mast in the process.

This inauspicious beginning on the Magothy was followed, years later, by lessons better learned in my twenties on Galveston Bay aboard *Itledoo*. She was the first boat that was all my own—a little sloop seventeen feet from stem to stern, wide as a bathtub in the middle, with an outboard motor no bigger than a blender hung off the transom. Then a junior associate at a large law firm in Houston, I would arrive at the office each Monday to face questions from a senior partner who kept a thirty-seven-foot luxury sailboat at the most prestigious yacht club on the bay. "Get out on the water this weekend, Hurley?" he would ask. The answer was invariably yes, followed by tales of hopscotch voyages north and south aboard *Itledoo*, wave-rocked anchorages, mishaps, and storms. All of this seemed the utmost in derring-do compared to his own weekend, usually spent in the slip and never far from the ice machine, where most big yachts remain most of the time. A legendary long-distance sailor and favorite author of mine, Hal Roth, described such boats, nodding ever at their docks, as "distant Tarzan yells" attesting to the virility of their A-type owners who toil in faraway office towers and dream of the South Seas, where they never go. I had such dreams, too.

On my way home from another utterly forgettable deposition in Beaumont, Texas, in 1986, on one of those interminably long, flat stretches of East Texas highway punctuated by the occasional Stuckey's restaurant, an idea occurred to me. My wife and I were in our twenties, with no children. We had law school finally behind us and student loan payments we could easily defer. I was content but not wedded to the idea of toiling to make partner at my firm. I had by then learned enough about sailing on our 1981 Cape Dory 30 cutter, *Anne Arundel*, to keep her right side up. It would be the perfect opportunity, I thought, to sell up and sail, stretch our legs, spend some time in the islands, and do what-have-you.

I don't recall exactly why we didn't go or whose idea it was to stay, but that's not important anymore. What is important is that we didn't go. We chose instead to make a home and rise in the ranks of our profession. It was the right choice. Far greater blessings followed—namely, two: a son, and then, eighteen months later, a daughter. I reveled in my return to Toyland, once banished forever, but now led in again by the hand of my own child. We moved back east to be closer to family. I began a new law practice in a small town in North Carolina and a new life as a father.

As soon as my children were old enough, in the mid-1990s, I started taking them on wilderness canoe trips and writing about those trips for publication. As they grew in age and experience, our maps became more distant and our destinations more daring, stretching into Canada and the Great North. I was a boy escaping into the woodlot again, but now I had the wherewithal to show my own children the far-flung adventures I had only dreamed of having as a child. Over an eight-year period, one or both of my children usually accompanied me on monthly wilderness expeditions, some lasting a week at a time, spanning more than fifty rivers and lakes all across America and two Canadian provinces. Those halcyon days for my children would change as all childhoods do, though in ways that neither they nor I could have imagined at the time.

In 1998, I left small-town life on the North Carolina coast and moved the family to Raleigh at the invitation of a large defense firm that needed an experienced litigator. Suddenly I was back in a fast-paced, corporate world after a ten-year sabbatical in my own small practice. During our first few years in Raleigh, I continued taking paddling trips with my children while also working full-time as a lawyer. By 2004, however, my children were becoming teenagers whose time and interests were naturally more inclined toward friends and sports teams than camping trips with Dad. It was just as well, as my own attention was increasingly drawn to the demands of the law firm. I left the wilderness and stopped writing. My practice exploded in size. The pace of life began to accelerate, and details of the passing daily scene seemed to blur as they went whizzing by. On the other side of that blur, I came to the end of a twenty-five-year marriage.

Chapter 4

A Voyage Lost

I was determined not to write even obliquely about the failure of my marriage, and I strove in various fits and starts, over months, to find an honest way not to do so. After all, a marriage is a two-sided story told differently by two people and clearly understood in all its particulars by neither.

I write of these things now because the end of my marriage is the crucible out of which this voyage and this memoir have come. It is my hope that by exploring the insights gained from this new perspective, I will have something important to say. Others will be the judge of my efforts, but it is important (to me) that I try.

William Maxwell once wrote, "When we talk about the past, we lie with every breath we take." If nothing else, I wish to prove him wrong in what I have to say now. While the problems in my marriage—as in all marriages—were a shared responsibility, the blame for the failure of my marriage is mine alone. I had an affair.

It is, somehow, too easy to write those words. Words cannot convey the enormity of what occurred. Worse, there is a self-congratulatory air to public confession and a false piety that comes from making a show of one's contrition. I don't have any illusions about my own piety, nor do I feel an impulse to congratulate myself for anything. Quite the contrary.

I have long been haunted by the words I wrote in an essay about marriage that was published in the fall of 1998:

> Over the long haul, there will come a cold, sober moment when all that separates us from the abyss of self-indulgence is the power of the promise we have made to each other. From our commitment to obey the promise in that moment—if for no better reason than because it is a promise—comes a wife's trust and the sound sleep of little children. From that trust comes the freedom to celebrate each other's differences without fear of being divided by them. And in that freedom abide the peace, joy and contentment we have been searching for all along.

I received more mail about that essay than almost any other. As powerful as those words were, I recognize in them now a warning to myself as much as an exhortation to others. At the time, the differences in my marriage had increasingly become, for me, a source of tension rather than celebration. Yet as a latchkey child of divorce, I had always promised myself that I would never put my own children through that hardship. In an effort to constrain my unease that our differences would one day divide us, I decided to "double down" on my promise to my wife by writing boldly about it to thousands of people. By those words, which I knew then to be true and still believe today, I had hoped to shame myself into commitment.

But I discovered that I had no shame. On a warm November day in 2005, I ignored every warning I had given to myself and others, and I leaped headlong into the abyss.

Like a drunken tourist racing to board a flaming, sinking ship bound for Disneyland, I convinced myself that I had found bliss in stolen moments with a married woman who shared my love of the outdoors and my impaired sense of judgment. It was a lie, of course, as all affairs are. It was also an act of unfathomable cruelty to the people affected most by my actions.

I have no intention, in writing this, that friends should lift me up and say, "There, now. Don't be so hard on yourself." I am quite capable of doing that on my own. I well know that infidelity is not as rare as we might think or hope. The idea—now so prevalent in law and politics—that there are "good" people and "bad" people and that "good" people always do the right thing is a fiction of the childish mind. The wisdom of country songs notwithstanding, every one of us, since the Fall of Man, has been the "cheating kind" in whatever area of life holds for us the greatest temptation. Humility requires that we understand this, but it is more important to know that we are not defined by our mistakes. A ship's wake tells you where she has been, not where she is going.

I have often considered that Christ, who surely knew that Peter would one day deny and betray him, gave him the keys to the kingdom anyway. He did not define Peter by his weakness, nor should we so define ourselves. Indeed, to wallow in self-opprobrium is arrogance worse than the sin because it values self-esteem and the esteem of others—which we often seek but so rarely find—more highly than God's forgiveness, which we rarely seek but already possess.

I am a firm believer in the power of grace, and even in the darkest of those days, when I had completely lost my way, I felt that God was near. Over the course of several weeks, I experienced the patient teaching of a nun who, though never married, had remarkable skills as a marriage counselor. At first begrudgingly and in the end very thankfully, I came to understand that affairs are not flights of romance between two soul mates but tragedies of self-delusion between two addicts. That understanding, however, for all its healing power in my own life, could not undo the damage I had done.

The affair finally ended, but my wife had the clarity of mind to see the obvious as well as the courage I lacked to admit it. In September 2006 she asked me to go, and by the next month I was gone. I returned to her door a year later, after rushing into dating and a string of failed relationships, to ask for her forgiveness and reconciliation. Both were refused, and none would say without good reason.

I did not linger. I learned, as the song says, that "everybody's got to leave the darkness sometime." After a year of separation, I found a divorce support group I wished I'd found on day one. I joined a men's Bible study group. I talked to someone older and wiser than I who convinced me to stop dating long enough to recognize my self-destructive pattern of seeking emotionally unavailable partners. I read books about boundaries. I found humility, yes, but also the courage to stand up for myself. I struggled, fell backward, tried again, and made slow progress.

It had been almost three years since I had left my marriage when I stepped off that airplane in Baltimore to find the *Gypsy Moon* and take her to sea. In that time I could be proud of one thing—I had not returned to the woman with whom I'd had the affair. But other than this one small triumph, my life had been altered in ways unforeseeable to me three years before. I battled loneliness, feelings of failure, my children's loss of trust, and the absence of friends once dear to me. My billable hours declined at work. Less than a year after my divorce was final, I suffered a second divorce when I was unanimously voted out of the partnership in the law firm where I'd spent the past eleven years. I found myself, at the age of fifty-one, back in solo practice, struggling to get a business loan in the worst credit market since the Great Depression.

When I lost my job, my income went to zero and then slowly recovered—as my new practice got underway—to less than half of what it had been before. I was one of the lucky ones who found work, but to ensure that I could meet alimony, child support, and tuition payments, I sold my house, my car, and whatever else anyone would buy. I moved into an apartment and found myself washing clothes in a communal laundry next to college kids in backward baseball caps and flip-flops, with the smell of marijuana wafting down the hall. There was a kind of gallows humor to it all. It wasn't poverty or hardship by any means, but it was transformational to me.

Even as the chips fell steadily lower, the *Gypsy Moon*—an aging sloop badly in need of major repairs and new sails—remained. Aside from the fact that no one would buy her in a down economy, her worth to me was measured more in dreams than dollars. She was a magic carpet, with a hull still "as hard as a New York sidewalk" in the estimation of one surveyor, and well equipped for flights of fancy. She was my partner in the continuing quest I had begun as a boy on Chesapeake Bay. She was a tangible reminder that despite all that had occurred to make my life so much smaller, there was still a reason to dream big dreams and a means to attain them.

The fire we endure has a way of refining us and giving us a kind of rebirth. In time, new parts of my life eventually bloomed. As you read this memoir, you will learn of these blossoms and blessings, none of which would ever have appeared but for the fire in my life.

It was once famously said that Italy produced the Renaissance despite thirty years of war and struggle, while Switzerland had only the cuckoo clock to show for its many centuries of peace and harmony. Despite the struggles I faced, I well know that whatever comes of my efforts now is likely to be much closer to a cuckoo clock·than to Da Vinci, but perhaps it will be a better clock than I might otherwise have made, or at least one that can tell the time. Time will tell.

So you see, August 2009 was a place of pause in my life. A moment of slack tide—that quiet hour right after something huge and once inexorable has been spent and just before something altogether new begins to move in another direction entirely. Whether such a time is the calm before the storm or that darkest hour before the dawn is a thing we can know only after we are carried off in it, as the tide waits for no man. But whatever it was, and wherever it was going, on that sunny afternoon near Annapolis, Maryland, I was not about to miss it.

Chapter 5

PREPARATIONS FOR SEA

The Gypsy Moon had undergone various repairs and improvements in preparation for the contingencies of an extended voyage, the need for some of which I had come to appreciate the hard way. Two years earlier, during her maiden voyage to the Bahamas, she had brushed shoulders with Tropical Storm Barry as it moved across Florida on the second of June—the first time a cyclone had come so close to those islands so early in the season in four decades. Wandering in the Abacos, far from VHF weather-radio broadcasts, I was caught unaware by remnants of the passing storm. As I made a run across fifty miles of open water from Great Sale Cay for the harbor at West End, my headsail shredded in high winds, and the sheets fouled the roller furling. Unable to make sail or lower sail, I learned then the value of old-fashioned hank-on jibs that go up when you pull the halyard and come down the same way. So one of the first changes made to the *Gypsy Moon* in preparation for this solo voyage was the removal of the roller furling and the replacement of the head stay.

The decision to take down a $2,000 roller furling system and switch to hanked-on headsails was a nod toward the reliability of a simple nineteenth-century design over the convenience of modern technology. Roller furling became common in the early 1980s. It allows a helmsman, while seated in the comfort of the cockpit, to deploy or stow the headsail merely by pulling a line wrapped around a drum at the base of the forestay. The line spins the drum, the drum spins the forestay, and the jib—tucked into a groove in the forestay like a window shade—furls or unfurls as the forestay swivels, depending on the direction in which you pull the line.

On a pleasant day's sail on the bay, roller furling is a convenient thing to have. It eliminates the need to put down your gin and tonic to travel to the foredeck to raise or lower the headsail. In a rising wind on the open ocean, however, with the risk of the line fouling in a rat's nest in the drum and the helmsman unable to retrieve or lower a flogging headsail, it is (in my opinion) of little convenience at all. Moreover, the thin fabric of sails appropriate for light winds is nothing like the cardboard-thick storm jib needed for heavy weather. You can't accomplish that sail change with roller furling. You've got to get your fanny on a pitching, wet foredeck, pull one sail down, and replace it with the other. Roller furling makes that process harder because it requires the sail to be fully unfurled before it can be lowered. Unfurl a three-hundred-square-foot sail in a thirty-knot squall and you're not likely to see it again soon. As a result, skippers on boats with roller furling often succumb to laziness in making sail changes too late, too infrequently, or not at all. They usually end up flying too much or too little canvas in high winds, which may explain why so many boats with roller furling that venture offshore are reported to suffer dismastings. And yet the pressures of modern marketing have done so much to make these and other "improvements" standard on new boats that seem more like floating RVs than seagoing vessels.

Another modification on the *Gypsy Moon* that went against the grain was the installation of a Monitor Windvane. This is a Rube Goldberg contraption that steers a boat on a constant heading relative to the wind, without benefit of electricity or fuel or human effort. It operates by means of a wind vane mounted on the transom. The vane is attached to a servo-pendulum rudder that pulls one of two lines running to the ship's wheel. As the boat veers off course, the vane backs against the wind, pushing the servo-pendulum rudder, which pulls the line, which turns the wheel, which alters the course of the boat until the vane is headed dead into the wind again. Monitor Windvanes are expensive to install and difficult to learn to operate correctly, but once mastered they can sail a boat on a straight course indefinitely. First perfected in the 1950s by some British "yotties" who were trying to race each other solo "across the pond," some form of this device has been a trusted ally on sailing circumnavigations ever since.

Push-button electronic navigation systems that operate by battery power are more commonly seen, and the *Gypsy Moon* is fitted with one. They are convenient and simple to operate, but they cannot handle the strain of heavy seas or high winds or constant use over a long span of time. The motors burn out or the gears strip. Simpler is better, most of the time.

High on the list of improvements was a newly inspected and repacked four-man inflatable life raft, which I nicknamed *Lucky Jack* after the hero of Patrick O'Brian's novels. It is stored in a sealed canister and strapped into a steel cradle that is bolted to the deck just ahead of the mast. The raft (I am instructed) deploys automatically when the canister, secured by its tether to a strong fitting on deck, is thrown overboard. The tug of the tether pulls a pin inside the canister that fires a CO_2 cartridge, which inflates the raft. The covered raft is designed for survival in all sea states, until help arrives. *Lucky*

Jack is well named because he has never been needed, and I for one am hoping his luck holds.

Other doomsday devices that I keep aboard include two Emergency Position Indicating Radio Beacons (EPIRBs), which, with the flip of a switch in a moment of need, will transmit an electronic signal embedded with the *Gypsy Moon*'s unique data signature and GPS coordinates to satellites in space from any ocean in the world. The satellites relay the SOS signal and the boat's exact position to the US Coast Guard and international rescue agencies.

Chapter 6

A Time to Go

So much for preparation and visions of disaster. This is, after all, a sailing voyage and not a moon launch. It is easy to get so carried away with the logistics of planning that we lose sight of what remains, which is simply "to go." On this subject Joshua Slocum, who in 1898 at the age of fifty-four became the first man to sail alone around the world, had this to say in the closing paragraphs of the book he wrote about his famous voyage:

> To young men contemplating a voyage I would say go. The tales of rough usage are for the most part exaggerations, as also are the stories of sea danger...Dangers there are, to be sure, on the sea as well as on the land, but the intelligence and skill God gives to man reduce these to a minimum. And here comes in again the skillfully modeled ship worthy to sail the seas. To face the elements is, to be sure, no light matter when the sea is in its grandest mood. You must then know the sea, and know that you know it, and not forget that it was made to be sailed over.

A Time to Go

I eased the *Gypsy Moon* away from the dock where she had been laid to after launching. The diesel engine kept up a low, steady rumble until I reached the last marker on the Magothy River. When I could feel the wind of Chesapeake Bay on my face, I pulled the kill switch on the engine and raised the headsail, as the world returned to silence. I was off, though only briefly, for the short sail to the mouth of the Severn River, where I would turn into Annapolis for the night.

As I glided into Spa Creek by the naval academy, my anchor found the bottom with plenty of sea room. I made the rode snug on the bow chocks. The boat turned smartly to the wind and luffed sail. Within minutes, all sheets and canvas were made fast. I was looking at Annapolis from the same place where Franklin, Jefferson, and Washington had viewed the town. They came here under sail, and so did I. Whatever poetry there was in that, I savored it only briefly before the heavens opened with a warm summer rain.

Annapolis Harbor may be crowded and the town may be overrun with tourists, but I have always enjoyed the convenience of its well-run water taxi service. Hailing a pontoon boat with a canopy to come alongside and take you from your anchored boat to the town dock, for the price of a few dollars, beats wrestling a dinghy onto the foredeck, inflating and launching it, and rowing it ashore—especially because the funds available for the repair of the *Gypsy Moon* had not included money for a suitable dinghy. Her last tender had disintegrated under the Bahamian sun two years earlier.

But the comforts of the water taxi extend only to the shoreline. Before I knew it, I was less in need of a dinghy than of a good set of weathers as the rain intensified. Running and dodging barhoppers from one sidewalk awning to the next in the sudden downpour, I finally arrived at Fawcett Boat Supplies in hopes of finally replacing my dime-store vinyl rain gear with the latest technical offshore racing duds. Alas, Fawcett's has always been extremely proud of their foul-weather gear, and I found the prices no different that night. I settled for some waterproof charts instead, and a waterproof tube in which to carry them. The captain would have to get wet.

Feeling like a cat scolded with a garden hose, I arrived later that night, a sodden mess, at the door of Middleton Tavern. This is the very place where Jefferson, Franklin, and Washington came to dine not long after the Revolution, although with better clothing, I suspect. Even so, I had declared my own independence and lived through my own revolution of sorts, and I felt in some way a part of that honored tradition in that historic town that night.

I had plans to meet two old friends—a college fraternity brother and his wife—at Middleton's. He had been a groomsman in my wedding in 1981, and we had stayed in touch through the years. He'd followed me to the same law school in the Midwest, did exceptionally well there, and returned to the Washington, DC, office of a big, top-drawer law firm, where he worked long hours for his clients and reaped the rewards—as well as the stress—of life as a silk-stocking corporate lawyer. A few years younger than I, he had always been thin and in annoyingly good shape. I could not constrain my disbelief when he told me, at dinner, of his recent heart attack. This was a young man. But he was characteristically upbeat and well versed in the medical science that now required even more careful attention to diet and exercise. In that moment I had the palpable sense that I was leaving on this voyage not a moment too soon and perhaps a good deal later than I realized.

We suppose that when pivotal moments in our lives finally arrive, they will be accompanied by the sound of trumpets on high or some outward epiphany of inner clarity. For me, nothing in my surroundings seemed different at all when I raised the anchor on that Sunday morning in August. My head was still in a fog of sleep when I began a voyage that would change my life forever.

Starting an ocean voyage is like asking a pretty girl to dance. There is nervousness and apprehension at first. When leaving for any length of time or traveling any distance, there is inevitably a feeling, at the beginning, that it all must be a terribly foolish undertaking, which you suppose is the reason why none of your wiser friends is aboard. But as master and vessel take their turns in the dance, as one leads and another follows, the dancers acquire a reassuring rhythm, and man and boat settle into the voyage as one.

There was barely a puff of wind, and within an hour of heading out of Annapolis, bound for the open ocean alone, I scarcely felt like Magellan. The flies were running circles around my boat. After a full day of sailing, I anchored in a cove still forty miles north of Hampton Roads, unable to catch any sleep under sail in the busy shipping lanes of the lower bay.

There wasn't a whisper of sound after I tucked the *Gypsy Moon* into her snug anchorage that first night. I was the only boat around but for a few crabbers coming and going far off in the distance. The lights in the windows of houses onshore gave off a soft glow, and I imagined that families inside were sitting down to dinner. I missed my own family. It is in just these still, calm moments when the naysayers of conscience seem to arrive. They disturbed my mind that night with rude criticism: "What are you doing here all alone? Do you notice that no other boat is anchored out in this godforsaken place tonight? Don't you suppose there's a reason for that? All the boats are in their slips, and their owners are with their families, getting ready to go to work tomorrow, where you should be. When are you going to grow up? Why must you always be looking over the horizon? Trust me, you're no Magellan. Besides, it didn't work out so well for Magellan, either. Or Columbus, for that matter. Give up this nonsense and put the boat into Norfolk or, better yet, put her up for sale and take up golf, like normal men your age. You're going to regret this, mark my words..." And so on.

The criticism got a good bit louder the following morning. I hit the snooze button and slept later than planned, but I was up like a rocket when I heard the noise of sails flogging in a sudden thunderstorm. Bolting out on deck in my skivvies, I felt the wind come in cool gusts from the southwest. It had caught a corner of the headsail stowed on the foredeck and had raised it halfway up the forestay. The sheets were snapping at me like a cat-o'-nine-tails as I tried to grab the flailing sail and tamp everything down on deck. When I finally won the battle and the storm had passed, I sat for a long moment in the cockpit. The naysayers returned to my thoughts. I knew why: I was coming to a point of decision. If I weighed anchor, I would be committing to the voyage offshore. I was scared already, and the storm hadn't helped matters, but whenever I thought of turning back, an awful sadness—almost an ache—welled up in my gut. There was something about this voyage that already owned me. I had to go. The idea of turning back seemed like a psychic death, a defeat, a resignation to an unkind fate. I raised the sails, and soon the *Gypsy Moon* and I were off again.

The Chesapeake Bay is a long, long thing. It was nightfall before I passed over the bridge-tunnel at Cape Charles and finally faced the ocean again. I had sailed many nights in the Atlantic before, but never alone, and never here. As I came through the shipping channel, the first difference I noticed was the slow, rhythmic rise and fall of the *Gypsy Moon* as she rode over the long swells rolling in from far out at sea.

At the mouth of the bay several shipping lanes converge, and in the night sky the navigation lights of huge freighters scarcely reveal their true size until they pass abeam, silently and slowly, like giant elephants tiptoeing into the harbor. The *Gypsy Moon* was entitled to the same navigational privileges as any other sailing vessel, but not being so restricted in her ability to maneuver, she owed a duty of deference to these behemoths in the close quarters of a channel. I knew, too, that like a mouse under their feet, my little ship would make them nervous with any sudden, unexpected change of course. I did my best to keep a careful heading toward the first waypoint, well out to sea and down the coast near Virginia Beach.

Very soon, it seemed, all the channel markers were behind me, and all that was left was the inky black of the night sky. The occasional crackle on the radio of the coast guard sector in Hampton Roads reminded me that I was not very far from where I'd started two days earlier. The sails were set for a gentle beam reach on a starboard tack, and the electronic autopilot whirred distractedly in short bursts, every few seconds, to keep the *Gypsy Moon* on course. I calculated the distance to my next marker as the lights onshore faded to starboard, set my bunk alarm for ten-minute intervals, and with the heel of the boat to port keeping me snug in the pilot berth, drifted off to what, over the next four days, would pass for sleep.

Chapter 7

WHISTLING IN THE GRAVEYARD

Diamond Shoals was my biggest worry. I don't know why, exactly. I had never been there before. It marks an area just off Hatteras Island where, spreading south along the Eastern Seaboard, the ocean floor suddenly rises up in sandy shoals to ensnare and swallow the keels of passing ships. Of the many ghost stories about the banks, one from Diamond Shoals had stuck with me. It told of a young woman aboard a passenger freighter that had run aground at night there in the nineteenth century. Terrified, she stood by the rail holding her infant child as the pounding surf rapidly broke the ship apart. One giant wave overtook them and, in an instant, swept the baby from her arms into the churning chaos of the night sea.

It was night when I arrived at Diamond Shoals, and the ocean was what any writer would feel compelled to describe as eerily calm—eerie like a murderer's smile. This is a place so long associated with violence and death that even in placidity, it cannot escape its legend.

Legend or not, I could plainly see the hazard on the chart: an area of shallow water, now clearly marked by a buoy with a flashing red light that had replaced various earlier lightships and structures used to mark the shoals. Most of these had sunk or been swept away in storms over the years. It seems as if it should be child's play to avoid the shoals in our GPS age, with a bright blinking light out in the darkness telling us where not to go. In fact, one sailor who read a newspaper account of my voyage asked me whether all that was needed to safely navigate the shoals was not simply to "go around it"—true, but not so simple.

What makes Diamond Shoals and all of the Outer Banks the Graveyard of the Atlantic is the Gulf Stream. The stream comes close inshore as it passes the banks and collides with colder waters from New England. Moving at a constant speed of two to four knots, the stream kicks up big seas most of the time, and enormous seas whenever waves carried by the current are opposed by a north wind. In fair weather, the combination of the current and the waves impedes a sailing vessel from making headway to the south within the stream—like trying to go up a down escalator. In foul weather, the issue is not making headway, but surviving.

There are two ways to avoid the Gulf Stream. One is to sail directly across it at something less than a right angle until you're a hundred miles or so out into the open Atlantic, then turn south. That's a fine plan if you're headed to the West Indies and don't need to cross the stream again to make port. If you're headed anywhere on the East Coast, you will prefer to sail right down the coastline, inshore of the western edge of the stream. In most places from Maine to northern Florida, you'll have anywhere from fifteen to forty miles of sea room in which to travel between the current of the stream and the shallows onshore. At Diamond Shoals, that margin thins to fewer than three miles in some places—a veritable bowling alley where rolling a gutter ball can be deadly.

I didn't fully understand all the foregoing particulars until my night alone on Diamond Shoals that August. I was happy to be cruising well out to sea, far from the storied dangers of the banks, with the wave-swept young woman ever in my mind's eye. But as I came farther south from Virginia, I felt the boat making slower and slower progress. At first, I assumed the wind had died, but when it became apparent that it had not, I realized that I was being carried northward by the western wall of the Gulf Stream. I found it necessary to tack farther and farther inshore, until it seemed I could almost read by the light of the Diamond Shoals marker. I marveled at just how close to the shoals I had to come to escape the effects of the current. Here, I learned, is where the devil and Diamond Shoals must be given their due.

Run aground on these banks at night in a storm, and help will be far from you. Your boat will lie on its side while the surf steadily pounds it to a wreck. That is why I love the open ocean: there is nothing to run into and no place to run aground. In fact, there are few things more frightening to a sailor in the dark than the sound of a clanging bell on a channel buoy or ocean waves hitting a beach, because both signal an unseen impending disaster. (Incomprehensibly, these are two of the "soothing" sounds programmed by the manufacturer into a clock radio that I own, along with thunderstorms and a babbling brook, presumably to help people sleep. I turn them on whenever I want to stay absolutely awake.)

I had not made much distance by the following morning. Looking back over the starboard rail, I could see the now-abandoned platform of an old light station rising from the ocean, atop Diamond Shoals. Like a haunted house in the daytime, it looked less frightening—though perhaps only because I was sailing safely away from it.

Chapter 8

LANDFALL BEAUFORT

Distances at sea can be deceiving. Although I was back in North Carolina waters, I was, on the morning after my passage around Diamond Shoals, still far from port. Beaufort, North Carolina, was where I planned to lay the *Gypsy Moon* over in a slip for what remained of hurricane season until she and I could be off again, by Thanksgiving.

Diamond Shoals was not the only mudbank of concern in these parts. It was nightfall before I approached the northern end of Cape Lookout, which protects Beaufort from the sea. Unlike the nightmares told of Cape Hatteras, the stories I associate with Cape Lookout are more familiar to me and more ordinary. More than once have I sailed into the bight at Cape Lookout and enjoyed a peaceful summer afternoon with dozens of anchored boats and hordes of tourists who come by land to see the old checkered lighthouse that stands there. But I had never approached Cape Lookout from offshore.

There would be no hazard for me at Cape Lookout, but I must confess I was unprepared to witness the wall of green water that I saw curling in one milelong wave after another, marching ashore on the ocean side of the cape. I mentioned it to friends later and was informed that Cape Lookout is prized by surfers. I can well understand why. From the *Gypsy Moon's* position at sea, beyond the shoals, the waves seemed more like rolling fields than water. The "bigness" of that place in the ocean impressed me, and I should think I would almost rather be skirting Diamond Shoals than trying to round that cape in a storm. Thanks, though, to the wonders of modern weather forecasting, I had occasion to do neither.

Upon spotting the outer markers of Beaufort channel from my position at sea, I felt a little like the Tin Man running through poppies to the Emerald City. It was seemingly just over the rainbow, but after hours of sailing, the shore remained elusively distant. By the slow application of wind to canvas, I eventually found the harbor, but not until nightfall.

A kind voice over the radio at Town Creek Marina, in Beaufort, gave me careful directions through the serpentine channel, as I would be arriving in the dark—long after the marina staff had gone home. The channel is bordered in some areas by water not more than inches deep, and great care is needed to avoid running hard aground. Feeling every inch a Down Easter, I found my way to the fuel dock at Town Creek and came alongside for the night. By the next morning, I was back in my office in Raleigh, in the world of suits and ties, lawyers and judges, deadlines and discovery, and other duties too numerous to mention. But I was better for the voyage, and I planned to continue at the first opportunity that work and weather might permit.

LATITUDE 34.72.64 N

LONGITUDE 76.47.61 W

BEAUFORT, NORTH CAROLINA

Chapter 9

A HOMECOMING

There is a God. Of this I was sure when I was a child, and this I know to be true today. The knowledge of Him is written in our hearts. Our every breath, our every joy and sorrow, and every element of the physical world, from its otherwise inexplicable existence to its well-ordered symmetry, fairly shout His name. That we have ears with which to hear this sound and minds with which to conceive that it is God who speaks to us is yet a further call to belief. But this belief, however certain, brings us only to the edge of a vast sea. From there, all else we yearn to know of God lies hidden and awaiting our discovery, on a voyage that each of us must make through the forbidding latitudes of faith and doubt, history and myth, hope and despair.

It is a strange journey that one begins by heading home, but that precisely describes the first leg of this voyage. The early spring of 2008, more than a year before this voyage began, was for me a time of emotional drift. It was then that I had brought the *Gypsy Moon* from North Carolina to Maryland at the reassuring invitation of family and old friends. My boat found a snug resting place in Annapolis Harbor. Those waters became an anchorage during the storms raging in my personal life at the time, and a distant refuge to which I often escaped. But Maryland was no longer my home.

From that northern offing, the voyage that is the subject of this memoir began. Thus it was that after sailing the first three hundred miles, I found myself in the fall of 2009 closer to home than when I'd started. Beaufort, North Carolina, where the *Gypsy Moon* came to rest after the first leg, is a mere day's sail from the sheltered harbor of New Bern, near the mouth of the Neuse River. New Bern is the first place in North Carolina where I had chosen to live, in April 1992. How I got there is the story of another epic journey in the small contours of my own life.

In 1984, at age twenty-six—newly minted by a Jesuit law school that had taught me more questions than answers—I struck out for Texas to find fortune and glory in the burgeoning litigation mills of Houston. Fortune, however modest by the standards of my peers, I did indeed find. But eight years into a legal career, with the birth of my second child, my notions of glory shifted, and the bloom fell off the Texas yellow rose.

With two babies in my charge, I woke up one morning in Houston to the realization that I was far from family and out on the frontier of a place very different from the one I had known growing up. I longed for the smell of balsam and spruce; for fiery red maples on crisp fall days; for city sidewalks and stone cathedrals; for green mountains; for old neighborhoods filled with two- and three-story houses; and for cohesive communities with roots as deep as the American Revolution. All of that may sound a bit odd to some, but when you have been reared an arm's length from taverns and meeting halls where the Founding Fathers knit together the fabric of our freedom, everywhere else has a temporary air. I felt the interloper in

Texas. The scrub-brush savannahs and desolate coastlines just didn't seem permanent to me.

I longed not only for different earth beneath my feet but, perhaps most of all, for the blue water and bracing shores of the Atlantic. Where it meets the upper Texas coast, the Gulf of Mexico is a gray, tepid backwater, not an ocean. But whatever the reason for my malaise, having young children who stood most to benefit from living closer to extended family made me feel this sense of isolation all the more acutely. We resolved to move back east.

A woman and her husband took over the reins of my law practice in Houston, and my wife and I left on a twelve-hundred-mile road trip in a weary Volvo with a weary baby girl crying in the backseat. Her animated big brother in the front would occasionally offer cheerful reassurances (which she was not buying) that this would all be "fun." It most certainly was.

I had a modest stake from the sale of my law practice with which to buy a small house in New Bern and start what I thought would be a bold new venture in the sailboat charter business. I knew that I would be eligible to receive a North Carolina law license after a six-month waiting period, but it didn't occur to me that returning to the practice of law would be at all necessary. The coast guard had given me an examination and a license as a boat captain. We lived simply, and for a short while, I plied my new trade to adventurous hotel guests and romantic couples aboard a twenty-eight-foot sloop that I had trucked up from Texas along with our furniture and other belongings.

Even at a speed of four knots, I sailed very quickly into the stern face of reality. Within a month my error was clear. North Carolina was not Maryland, and New Bern was not Annapolis in the making. The sailing tradition that I had known in my youth was not deep in the culture there. In the Old South, rivers were places where people dumped used tires, dead bodies, and everything else they were either ashamed of or didn't know what to do with. When I arrived, it had not been that long since the timely intervention of some far-sighted citizens had spared New Bern's now elegant and valuable riverfront from becoming the premises of the city jail.

Most boats in farming country, I found, were used for water-skiing and fishing, not quiet reveries. Many of the sailboats in New Bern were brought in by transplanted Yankees who were lured by cheap home prices to retire in the area. Some of these folks, judging by how often their boats left their slips, had grown too retired to sail them.

In my little sloop *Intrepid*, I was always, it seemed, alone on the river. The scenery was inviting. The estuaries that make up the North Carolina coast are more forested and their shorelines more secluded, even today, than those on the Chesapeake Bay to the north. A gentle wind blows across these wide lowlands with a constancy welcomed by sailors. Passengers from the North who chartered with me would marvel at miles and miles of open water without seeing a single sailboat underway. Eastern Carolina tobacco farmers came aboard with their wives to be stunned by the silence of a vessel that moved by wind (only to leave disgruntled that I would not let them smoke cigarettes, with ashes flying like bullets in the breeze through yards of expensive sailcloth).

I didn't make much money, but I did acquire the only real suntan this pale Irish skin has ever known. I also became a better sailor, though I retained a mystified ignorance of the sailboat diesel engine. I was then as I am today at the mercy of that holiest of high priests, the diesel mechanic, to exorcise the demons that seem so easily and regularly to possess that poor iron beast. For those services I have tithed generously at his altar.

By February 1993, I had been admitted and sworn into the North

Carolina Bar. Within two months of opening a one-room rented office, I once again had a small stable of paying clients and cases needing my attention. All of this happened just in time to salvage my family's finances from an impoverished income in the charter business that was not destined to improve.

In all honesty, I felt the fool and as though I had let my young family down by having given up a lucrative law practice in Houston for something that was, in hindsight, so seemingly adolescent as a one-man sailboat charter business. I did have bigger dreams, for what they were worth. I had actually imagined a little fleet of day sailors that would one day grow to include a retail import business. Someday, I thought, I might even have a three-masted schooner that traveled between the Carolinas and the Caribbean in the winter months, in a kind of a low-tech reprise of the West Indies spice trade that would also carry well-heeled American tourists as passengers. Instead, I found myself far from the West Indies, circling in the usual cul-de-sacs where ambition so often ends. I was reminded that it takes money to make money, that skill at running a law practice is not directly convertible into skill at running a business, and that the value of a dream to the dreamer and its value to others are different things. Not many members of the general public thought as I did. Most preferred lying on a beach over sailing to one. Others wanted to be on a fast boat or water-skiing behind it. Seasickness warded off all but a hardy few of the rest. In one year of effort I counted only 181 paying passengers.

Yet these were not hard times. In these years as in every year, no matter how little or great my income, no one in my family knew a moment of want. As for how this could be possible, "consider the lilies," we are told, and as simple as that sounds, it is wonderfully if not almost eerily true. This parable was the story of my own family's journey, but the lessons of that experience apply to everyone.

We are often timid and doubtful, reluctant to follow our dreams in so many areas of our lives. Looking back, I see that my plan to feed a family of four from a one-boat sailboat charter business was never a recipe for success, but I also see that there was nothing to fear in trying, nor any shame in failing.

The world has a way of working itself out, in my experience. There are things unseen. Life is not always easy or pleasant, and it is often unfair, but it seems to unfold according to some plan of which we are only peripherally aware—like a dream, the details of which are vivid only when we are sleeping. We cannot remember—much less comprehend—that dreamworld with the powers of a rational mind.

There are many who would bitterly object to any suggestion that "the world has a way of working itself out" as a simple-minded, romantic delusion. As one who has led a simple, romantic, and mostly charmed (if not deluded) life, I don't presume to question the validity of anyone's objection or insist that others join me in some sort of cheerful oblivion. But when people ask why, if God is truly in charge, their lives can go so badly awry or why horribly tragic things can happen to innocent people, I am reluctant to accept the premise of the question. At times when I might otherwise want to rail against God for His failure to intervene to prevent what I perceive as the gross injustice of this world, I am reminded of the plight of an infant at birth.

Within the limits of the infant's awareness, the birth pangs that are occasions of such joy to unseen others are to him a senseless crisis of unimagined proportions. His uterine world is literally collapsing around him. He has no capacity to understand that he is being delivered to a life of incalculably greater meaning, in a new world that expectantly awaits his arrival and already knows his name. He screams with anxiety and is slapped ignominiously, but his present pain is only a temporary hardship, destined soon to be utterly forgotten.

I believe that the heartache we experience in our journey in this world is much the same. I have sensed this truth many times in my own life. Others express it routinely in the idea that things happen—even things that seem senseless at the moment—for a reason. The existence of reason implies the existence of a reasoner.

I recall once hearing a television talk show host not best known for his humility and reticence say that he dismissed the whole notion of redemptive theology because it simply made no sense to him that God would need to bleed and die on a cross for our sins. Frankly, I share his incredulity. Even the church acknowledges that our faith is an inscrutable mystery ("Christ has died; Christ is risen; Christ will come again"); yet faith tells me that it is true. Humility allows me to accept by faith what I cannot know by reason or intelligence. What a small church it must be whose altar spans only the verities of the rational mind. The world is so very much bigger than that, and so likewise must be its creator.

It was good to be home, in Beaufort, when the *Gypsy Moon* glided to those docks in the gathering darkness of an August night in 2009. It was good to be back in North Carolina. It was good to be near New Bern, which held so many memories, both bitter and sweet. I had smiled inside, in those lonely hours spent ghosting down the coast in the darkness off Cape Hatteras, to hear US Coast Guardsmen pass the baton—their broadcasts changing from the clipped elocution of big northern cities to the relaxed drawl of little southern towns. The South is my home.

Though a child of Baltimore and an early admirer of certain refinements of northern life that forever eluded me—namely a well-placed shot in lacrosse and the rigors of piano lessons at the Peabody Institute—I had never much warmed to northern culture. Since my first visit to rural Tennessee, at the age of fourteen, I had recognized in southern folk a genuine sense of friendship and community—often mistaken for mere politeness—that was like mother's milk to me.

Yes, I like it here. That being so, it was not immediately clear, nor was it ever clear for very long, why I should leave on a half-baked sailing voyage for someplace else.

Chapter 10

AN UNLIKELY ADVENTURER

The matters of my departure from Beaufort and my ultimate destination were decisions yet to be made. I knew this in my heart to be true, even though I admitted it to no one and had set out from Annapolis amid great fanfare, with news to all that I was "bound for Nassau." Telling people you are sailing to Nassau—especially people who would never attempt such a trip themselves but are sure to be impressed that you would—is easy to do. It evokes an air of adventure, derring-do, sophistication, and romance. James Bond seduced beautiful women, danced at Junkanoo, and foiled diabolical plans for nuclear blackmail in Nassau. Telling people that you are sailing to Nassau when you are as yet in a harbor a thousand miles away is much like telling people that you are writing a bestselling novel or running for president. It is a thing much easier imagined than realized.

Actually sailing to Nassau, I would come to understand, is hard to do—not just in terms of time and distance but, for me, psychologically. The wind and the waves are not the only forces that must be overcome or even the most worrisome. The whole idea evoked in me assorted feelings of anticipation and dread, elation and dejection, self-satisfaction and self-doubt, resolution and regret.

Many people—perhaps you among them—have made voyages in comfort and safety to the Bahamas from the northeastern part of the United States in small boats sailing out of sight of land, without expecting a medal from the Seven Seas Cruising Association for their efforts. I know this. I don't mean to make a moon shot out of a mud puddle by my somewhat overwrought narrative. I do wish, though, to come clean and admit something: despite any pretentions to the contrary in the letters you now hold in your hands, I am not, nor have I ever been, a Salty Dog.

True Salty Dogs—those self-sufficient Lords of the Deep who write books on navigation and the finer points of sail trim and boat mechanics—have long been a source of intimidation and annoyance to me. As best I can tell, there is not a poet among them. They are math-science folk and engineering types all. For them a clogged fuel line, battery overload, or electrical malfunction is a thing of rapture, and they set about solving the problem with the kind of Yankee ingenuity and determination "that built this country, by jiminy." For me, however, these malfunctions are all signs from a benevolent God that man was meant to sail across oceans by the light of oil lamps, not motor across them with enough spare amps to power a refrigerator and a satellite weather station.

Yet the Salty Dogs are the men women long for, who, given only an axe and a pack of matches, could build them a shopping mall. Give me an axe and a pack of matches, and I'll build a woman a campfire around which to sing her a love song, neither of which will serve its intended purpose once it starts raining.

For starters, I am afraid of the ocean, although on this point any true sailor would readily concur. I have imagined an unmarked grave for myself beneath the waves many times, often out of a macabre boredom on long watches, but more often for the purpose of planning ways to avoid it. I am almost never sick at sea, thank God, but because my loved ones sometimes are, I have chosen to sail some of the rougher, longer passages alone. When I do, I often suffer bouts of loneliness and melancholy, although this comes with the benefit of encouraging sleep on long passages, perchance to dream of those whom I love and miss.

Once I settle into a voyage that takes me away from work and family, I continually question my judgment in having begun it and the wisdom, not to mention the expense, of continuing it. There has not been an extended voyage in memory in which I did not firmly resolve at some point to sell or give away the infernal boat at the nearest port and fade into a sensible life of gardening and bridge.

Yet despite my disconsolate temperament, ever have I heard the still, small voice that says "go." I cannot tell you why. I do not know. But I do understand what the message means. It is not an invitation or a compulsion to "go have fun." I know whose voice that would be: the same fifty-three-year-old lawyer who often tells me to go for that extra slice of birthday cake, or to settle into a DVD-induced haze on a couch in a dark, cozy room instead of riding a bike or picking up a book or writing this memoir to you.

People for whom sailing is a way to have fun, rather than a way of life, don't long for the horizon. What they seek can be found in a weekend club race or a day trip that ends back at the marina. People do not sail out of sight of land and endure the monotony of an unchanging sea for days on end, punctuated occasionally by the heart-thumping anxiety of storms and the uncertain contours of a distant landfall, far from aid, because it is fun. (Though to be fair, in many moments it is precisely that.) They sail because they know that the journey is its own reward, that it leads someplace beyond a mere geographical destination, and because they hear the call of Thoreau's different drummer to go wherever that might be.

The call to go is a yearning to peer behind the curtain that encircles and confines our world to the close, the familiar, and the safe. It is a call to strip life bare of its clutter and distractions and to reencounter the primal interest in the unknown that first led us to explore the other end of the crib. Somewhere along the way, most of us stopped exploring. Some of us did not. Some of us cannot.

One day this voice telling me to "go" will perhaps be diagnosed as a form of mental illness that I have suffered unawares, but for now it serves me well as an excuse to go sailing. It was, after all, no less a madman than Mark Twain who gave us these words:

Twenty years from now you will be more disappointed by the things that you didn't do than by the ones you did do. So throw off the bowlines. Sail away from the safe harbor. Catch the trade winds in your sails. Explore. Dream. Discover.

Chapter 11

WHAT DEAN MARTIN KNEW

I have gotten somewhat ahead of myself in the story of this voyage. Before the moment of decision at Beaufort in the fall of 2009, there was another longing, and another unfinished voyage awaiting the order to set sail.

Gary Chapman has written a wonderful book, *The Five Love Languages*, in which he makes the case that each of us is hardwired to recognize and appreciate love in one or more well-defined ways. I have been, since my earliest memory, a person with a need for love in the languages that Chapman describes as "words of affirmation" and "physical touch," in that order. In less clinical terms, that means that I am rather insecure and need lots of attaboys and hugs. Despite this, I have had an unfailing instinct for cultivating relationships certain never to meet those needs.

Sooner or later, we all have to come face to face with the people we truly are, and so did I—albeit rather late in the game and amid the financial and emotional wreckage of a bruising divorce. What I learned in the process was invaluable to me in trying to repair my life. Little did I know that the Rolling Stones had figured all this out before, if only I'd been listening.

Yes, it's true. You can't always get what you want. We all need to accept that, and grown-ups generally do. But you darn well better get what you need, or you may find that your needs are being met in unhealthy ways in other parts of your life. That certainly happened to me, and with disastrous and painful consequences.

But as surely as winter leads to spring, pain is followed by healing and growth. I came to realize several truths, not all of them in step with the pop psychology of the day, as I set out on a quest to find love and happiness. I was looking for "the one."

First, I considered and rejected the current self-help orthodoxy that holds that it is unhealthy to need anything or anyone outside ourselves in order to feel emotionally whole. Only after we achieve a sublime indifference to the affections of others, this theory goes, will true love alight (or not) like a butterfly on our shoulders while we're busy finding fulfillment in pottery or poetry, meditation or mountain climbing, whale-saving or what-have-you. I generally didn't agree with this school of thought, mostly because the dull fellow it describes doesn't sound like someone I would ever want to be. (I also wasn't happy with the whole butterfly thing. If I'm choosing metaphors in the animal kingdom for an on-time arrival with my heart's desire, I'm going with a chicken hawk, not a butterfly.) And as for being perfectly content to be alone, I had always thought the Paul Simon song "I Am a Rock," was a lament, not a model of emotional wellness.

I much preferred the wisdom of Barbra Streisand that "people who need people are the luckiest people in the world," followed by no lesser light than Dean Martin, who told us that "you're nobody till somebody loves you." (Dino was exaggerating, admittedly, but we all still got the point.) The pop psychologists would have a field day with the codependency suggested by those lines, but I bet their songs would sell fewer records.

What Dean Martin Knew

Hoagy Carmichael wasn't fooling anyone when he wrote "I Get Along Without You Very Well," and that really wasn't his plan. We are made for community, both romantically and socially, and we know it. In case I have offended anyone's musical tastes, there's always Loggins and Messina, with their advice in "Danny's Song" that "if you find she helps your mind, better take her home..." There you have it: the Gospel according to Casey Kasem.

In truth, almost no one agreed with me in these ideas—least of all the women. After three years of separation and divorce, I found myself adrift in bachelorhood, no closer to shore than when I'd started, and beginning to feel the effects of the sun. I had perused hundreds of online dating profiles and begun to notice a pattern in what (usually divorced) women now in their forties and fifties are seeking in a man. It is more of a side salad than an entrée.

Most women described themselves as well satisfied and living a full and busy single life. They would pointedly warn that they were not looking for Mr. Right, but should he carelessly stumble across their path, he must be prepared to defer to what they would ominously warn would "always be" their "first priority." This was usually children, although in some cases it was extended family or a particular passion in life. The invitation to the hapless Lothario was clear: "If you hitch your wagon to my star, our relationship will never be at the center of my galaxy. We will spin in orbit around some other planet." I didn't want that, and I didn't agree with that.

These cheerfully written profiles were like billboards along a highway, intended to entice the weary traveler to take the next exit into someone's private world, but they read to me more like the warning sign to the Cowardly Lion in the Haunted Forest: I'D TURN BACK IF I WERE YOU.

Lest I be accused of stealing candy from babies, I hasten to add what a Catholic priest once told me. Couples going through the church's pre-Cana program to discern their readiness to marry, he said, invariably answer this question incorrectly: What should be your first priority, your relationship with your children or your relationship with your spouse?

The most common answer of prospective mothers and fathers is that their relationship with their children would certainly come first. In a way, this answer makes perfect sense. Children need love and nurturing to develop properly, and for a time during their development, their needs are so great and so constant that they must take precedence over the needs of husband and wife. Husbands and wives gladly make that sacrifice. I did. Very likely you did. There is no contest here.

It is also a fact of life that romantic love can fade and marriages can end, while the bond between a parent and child endures forever. Yet even the Catholic Church recognizes that when children revolve in orbit around their parents' relationship, they (and their parents) lead healthier lives than when children are made the center of their parents' universe.

An example from my boyhood better illustrates the point that millions of parents in my generation—and now the many divorced mothers among them—seem to be missing: I lettered in three sports in high school and played varsity lacrosse on a championship team in college, in the 1970s, and yet I cannot recall a single practice and no more than a handful of games that my mother ever attended. In fact, almost no one's mom or dad was ever at practice, and none of us minded—or noticed. We got there on our bikes or we walked, and if there was an away game, our parents took us only if we couldn't find a ride with a friend. My mother worked hard, and though I didn't give it much thought at the time, I'm sure she had better things to do than to spend what blessed free hours she had on a Saturday morning cheering wildly as though I had done something remarkable by catching a pass or running fast on twelve-year-old legs. Playing sports was, for me, all the reward I needed, and as a result I was self-motivated to play with a dedication that took me as far as my abilities allowed. No one ever handed me a juice box or a brownie at halftime, but the team had a bucket and (one) ladle with all the ice water we needed.

Years later, by the time I was coaching my son's middle school lacrosse team and his sister was participating in soccer and gymnastics, the world had dramatically changed. The players' parents—nearly all of them—were lined up like opposing armies along the sidelines for hours on end. Parking lots were choked with minivans. Parents were there not just for championship matches but for every game and most practices. The majority were there not just on a few weekends but every weekend. Some families sheepishly escaped during school breaks to go on vacation together, but many stayed home to attend practices as a sign of their "commitment to the team." Rotund mothers anxiously shouted strategic advice to their tiny daughters on balance beams. Brigades of parents descended on fields at halftime with a veritable banquet of delights. Although the majority of these kids would never play beyond the middle school level, hundreds of dollars were spent on high-end equipment, elite training camps, and private leagues that involved overnight travel, hotels, and a total commitment of the parents' time.

Something seems very wrong with this picture. But needless to say, I didn't try hard to win this argument in my own family, and our family was no different than most. I gave up and happily joined the throng. Kids naturally want to do what other kids are doing, and the same is true of parents. There is enormous social pressure not merely to conform to, but to excel at, generational norms of parenting. The baby boomers, my generation, have been the most hovering parents in history. This shows in the way it has shaped our children and our relationships.

Admit it: most kids today don't show nearly the same level of initiative and independence that you did at the same age. Adolescence, I am told, has been officially extended to age thirty. When husbands and wives make children the center of their lives and their marriage, either they become invested in the children's never really leaving (hence the phenomenon of lengthening adolescence) or, when the children do leave, the marriage withers like a hollow tree. It may stand, petrified, but only until a strong wind blows.

Chapter 12

A MOMENT OF INDECISION

So it was, I realized, as I strove to follow the advice of Streisand, Martin, Carmichael, Loggins and Messina, et al., that I was kicking against the goad. The problem is no longer that the glass slipper does not fit. It is that glass slippers have gone out of style, and Cinderella is likely to call the cops when the prince shows up.

I did not want to become anyone's side salad or fashion accessory, the missing piece of an already completed puzzle, or the consolation prize in someone's otherwise disappointed life. I met some wonderful women and even nearly lost my heart a time or two, but after three years of earnest effort I had found no one with whom I shared a dream of the future. As the close of hurricane season approached in the fall of 2009, I was a ship in irons, rolling around the sea in light airs and lacking a heading.

The Wednesday afternoon before Thanksgiving was a melancholy gray. It was growing dark and chilly by the time I left Raleigh for the three-hour drive to Beaufort. A call came in on my cell phone from a friend. She invited me to have Thanksgiving dinner at her home with her family. With no small difficulty, I declined. She insisted. I reconsidered.

The weather was downright depressing. Accepting an invitation for Thanksgiving dinner would have been a welcome excuse to put off the overnight sail offshore to Masonboro Inlet that I had planned. The next day's long trip was due to take me down the waterway to Southport, where I expected to dock the boat before jumping off for Nassau a week later. I was also afraid to set sail, to be honest.

It was not the dreary weather, or being alone, or the sixty-mile stretch of ocean from Beaufort to Masonboro Inlet that concerned me. On the open sea at night, the *Gypsy Moon* is as cozy as a warm fire and rocks like a baby's cradle as she rises and falls over the waves. It was the unknown that troubled me, and the worry that I was about to do something rather foolish (again) and potentially very expensive (again) that I would regret (again).

My life was hardly a pillar of constancy. I had been through some rough times. Money was an issue. I had a towering bill from my divorce lawyer that would take years to pay off and an eye-watering alimony payment to go with it that I would be making each month until my old age. My law practice was running smoothly enough, and I had carved out the time in my schedule to go, but if I stayed behind and worked I would make more money. There were a million reasons not to slip the lines and sail away from what seemed, then, a relatively safe harbor in my life.

To make my decision no easier, I had gotten a call from my old pals at Northwest Creek Marina, near New Bern, the week before. After I'd given up my slip in that idyllic spot two years earlier, when leaving on my first trip to the Bahamas, I'd returned to find that I was at the bottom of a waiting list of a hundred people hoping to put their boats where mine had been. The other marinas where I was forced to keep the boat instead, when I returned, charged more than twice as much. Now my old berth was open again. Bringing the boat back there would have seemed the logical thing to do. It was just a two-hour drive from my home in Raleigh, over good roads in a well-sheltered harbor with first-class repair facilities nearby, on a river I knew well—too well, in fact.

Harbors where every mark holds a memory and every face is an old friend are places best saved for old men and little children. "Not yet," I thought.

I arrived at the boat slip in Beaufort and went aboard. I found the *Gypsy Moon* as always, floating cheerfully high on her lines and listing ever so slightly to port, with dry bilges, clear decks, and everything in its place. Three teak hatch boards, varnished to a high gloss, enclosed the companionway. Removing them, I saw that all was in good order in the cabin below. There was a place for everything, and everything was in its place. The *Gypsy Moon* was not in Bristol fashion, by yachting standards. (She is, after all, a working boat, with all the attendant scuffs and scrapes.) But I would not have been embarrassed to serve the governor tea in my galley, had she been aboard.

I bent the genoa onto the forestay and ran the sheets aft, port, and starboard, through the running blocks. The mainsail was furled on the boom and ready. I examined the route I would take through the narrow channel that leads from the marina to the bascule bridge and past the town of Beaufort, established in the year 1709. Along the town's older streets, by the waterfront, a few brightly painted homes from those early years stand where they have witnessed the storms and worries of more than two centuries. But outside of a few historic avenues, little is left of the old places. Out on the main road, on my way into the marina, I passed a well-lighted orange Hardee's sign—an emblem of the New South that has overtaken the legacy of Colonial fishermen, merchants, and planters.

When all the work had been done to make ready for sea, I

paused. All of the questions and objections that I had kept waiting at the bar these past few months now demanded a hearing and a decision. Would I go? Should I go?

The harbor master's office and chandlery at Town Creek Marina are encircled by a wide covered porch on which the staff has thoughtfully placed a number of high-backed rocking chairs. I found one of these and took my place, looking out over the water to the south. I was alone. The harbor was dark. The intermittent light rain of the day had eased. I could see the lights of the low bridge, not a quarter mile away, and the now-thinning automobile traffic that rumbled across it. No one and nothing stirred in the marina. All was quiet and still, as though the assembled instruments of the harbor's orchestra had come to order, awaiting the rise of a conductor's baton.

I am not what most religious people would call a praying man, which is not to say that I do not often pray. I readily give thanks for all that has been given to me, which is mountainous, and beg forgiveness for my lack of faith, which is cavernous. It is rather that I feel a strong impulse toward formality, humility, and decorum when presuming to importune the Almighty.

Part of this attitude, I suppose, comes from my earliest years in the Episcopal Church, where purse-lipped communicants rarely break into spasms of ecclesiastical joy for all the world to see. Part of this also comes from my life in the law, where a lawyer's remarks to a judge are brief, to the point, made from a posture of respect, and mindful that the court's considerable power must not be invoked unadvisedly or for any trivial purpose. Most of my reticence in prayer, though, is owed to the knowledge that the winds that bear aloft my petitions carry with them the prayers of some poor soul with malarial fever, a father keeping vigil over a sick child, or a wife on the eve of a battle from which her husband may not return. I am

a well-fed lawyer playing about on a pleasure yacht, a stranger to illness and hardship, and a free man living in the most affluent nation
on Earth. I am ashamed to be a supplicant in their company.

And yet I pray, because that is what children do. Well do I know
that whatever I truly need, my Heavenly Father will grant, and that
the burden of what I truly deserve has been lifted through no merit
of my own.

I prayed that night, on the porch, for guidance in making a decision whether to go. I knew that I was committing myself to a
journey that would take not weeks or months to complete, but
years, and from which I or my boat might not return. I knew that
it would cost money—not an inordinate amount (the boat is paid
for, and the wind is free), but not an insignificant amount, either. I
wanted to go and felt that I should, but I knew from long experience
that I have wanted many things that I should not want, and that
my judgment has not always served me. My self-esteem and self-
confidence were not at a high ebb in that hour of my life. I wanted
guidance. I wanted fatherly advice.

There are some who say God speaks to them. I am not so sure.
He has spoken through the prophets, according to my creed, but He
has never spoken directly to me. I have, however, felt the presence of
God. And from the perspective of the higher altitudes that the passage of time affords, I have seen the influence of the Holy Spirit in
my life. All the same, I can't say that I saw, heard, or felt anything of
the kind, in the half hour I spent rocking and praying on the porch
at Town Creek Marina. It seemed that God was leaving this call up
to me, and so I made the best one I knew how to make.

If I was looking for a sign that I had made the wrong call, it would
not be long in coming. It was dark in the marina, for sure, but not
nearly so inky black as it was out in the creek. The markers in the
spur channel leading through the mud flats from the marina to the

main waterway were not lighted. I should have laid out a compass course to follow, but it seemed too short a distance to bother. It had been easy enough three months earlier, when I had arrived there in daylight.

Not one minute away from the dock, as I was making way under engine power toward the bascule bridge, I lost my bearings in the channel while looking down at a handheld GPS unit. I was having trouble finding my boat's position on the blasted display. When I looked up, I noticed the bottom shoaling quickly on the depth sounder. Thinking I must be to starboard of the channel, I swerved to port, then felt a sudden downward lurch at the bow and an unwelcome firmness at the stern that signaled I was aground.

I had nosed into the mud of Town Creek, having strayed out of the narrow and unforgiving channel in my eagerness to get underway. It must have been eight or nine o'clock when this happened, and on the eve of Thanksgiving, no less.

Emblematic of the efficiency of the American maritime industry that I was sure I would miss wherever I was headed, a towboat was on my location in twenty minutes. In ten minutes more, the tow had turned the nose of the *Gypsy Moon* a few yards in the right direction, and not fifteen minutes after that, I was gliding through the channel, talking on the ship's radio and saying thanks and good night to the bridge tender. There was nothing between me and the open sea.

Chapter 13

A Wanderer's Vigil

The seas at the entrance to Morehead City remind me of the inside of a washing machine most any day. Tide and season merely determine whether you're going to get the wash or the spin cycle. On this night, though, the waves rolled in long and slow, and the *Gypsy Moon* made her way gently out to sea. I chose a distant marker before making the turn to the south that would put me on a heading for Masonboro Inlet, at Wilmington. The winds were light from the northwest, and with her big drifter set out to port, the boat dipped her shoulder slightly and began the familiar jog that meant she was making good time on a broad reach.

Out on the ocean, there was not another ship as far as my eyes could see. The quarter moon was gone and so was the rain, but the clouds obscured the stars. I set the autopilot and kept up a watch in the cockpit until the lights from Atlantic Beach, just south of Morehead City, began to fade astern. With the bow pointed out to sea, all sheets running fair, and the sail pulling well, I set the egg timer above my bunk in the pilot berth to ninety minutes and closed my eyes.

There is something inherently holy about wandering, and that holiness enriches the wanderer so much that the voyage itself becomes the destination. In that first sacred hour of silence at sea, my thoughts collected around the decision I had just made, where I had been, and where I was going. It was hard not to notice that I was alone on a holiday set aside for families to gather around one another and give thanks. Although my solitude was self-imposed, it ran deeper than the mere proximity of people with whom I might have shared a meal and a laugh. It was impossible to overlook that I had come to a point in my life when I was, whether on land or at sea, truly, truly alone.

I had wanted my children to be with their mother and hadn't bothered to insist on a formal visitation schedule because they were already in high school when my marriage ended. But I wasn't prepared for how rarely I would see them. Although it was hard to determine how much of this was due to the alienation of divorce and how much was simply the norm, as teenagers with cars and friends and plans of their own begin to pull away from parents, the effect was the same.

I no longer had a job, it seemed, as a husband or a father. The powerful motivation those vocations supplied had accounted for virtually every success I had achieved since the age of twenty-three. They were jobs I had once done very well, but I was now unemployed in the most abject sense of the word. I wanted nothing so much as I wanted to "work" again.

My mind wandered to a church in Aspen, Colorado, where I had spent a chilly Saturday afternoon nearly three years before. It had been snowing all day in one of the snowiest seasons on record in Aspen. Some twenty-one feet had already fallen by late February of that year. I was due to fly home the next day. I am guessing that the pastor of St. Mary Catholic Church on Main Street thought he had a free hour on his hands when he trudged through the drifts to the church to keep his appointment for five o'clock confession, but there were three of us waiting for him that day. I was the last in line.

Having been married in the Catholic Church, taken instruction in the faith, and been confirmed some years later, I had been a practicing Catholic for eighteen years when my marriage ended. During that time I had served in various positions as chairman of the parish council, youth group director, CCD teacher, and a third-degree member of the Knights of Columbus. I felt a strong kinship to the Catholic faith, and after my divorce I wanted the reassurance of my church that I might one day remarry and still have a home there.

I made my confession to the priest about the affair that had ended my marriage. It was no accident that I had waited to do this in Aspen, Colorado. I was too ashamed to face anyone in my home-town. The sordid details would be made public not long thereafter in my divorce trial, but at the time I still felt like a man with a dark secret. My infidelity had its origins in the church.

The woman involved was the lay administrator of our parish. In a twist of irony that was not lost on anyone, her affair with me ended the affair she had been having with our parish priest, who then re-nounced his vows and left the priesthood, only later to renew those same vows and return to serve a different parish. The woman re-signed her job at our church, began attending a different parish, and stayed married to her husband. My marriage fell apart. It was a scan-dal and the greatest failure of my life.

The young pastor at St. Mary's in Aspen was very kind, almost apologetic, but firm. He made it clear to me that I had two options to remain in communion with the church. One was to stay single and celibate for the rest of my life and let my solitude be a testament to my piety. That certainly wasn't ringing any bells with me. I knew who I was, and I also knew that fifty years of solitude and celibacy would make my life a testament to nothing so much as the prolonged effects of clinical depression.

The other option, the priest explained, was for me to seek an annulment by proving to a tribunal in the church, through the testimony of family and friends, that my marriage of twenty-five years had never occurred in a heavenly sense, despite the two angels it had produced here on Earth.

Catholic guilt is a powerful thing, and I would later go so far as to meet with a diocesan counselor—a nun who was wonderfully kind and forgiving—to learn more about the grounds for annulment. After hearing the story of the fever of immaturity in which my marriage had begun at the age of twenty-two, this good nun appeared certain that an annulment would sail through, and I have no doubt she was right. But the more certain she appeared, the less interested I became.

There grew in me a sense of something self-righteous, sanctimonious, and even bullying about the whole idea of putting two impulsive kids—who were all wrong for each other but who couldn't see that twenty-five years ago—on trial. Great goodness came of their decision to marry, but so did great sorrow. Isn't that just a part of life? Isn't every marriage and every life a mixed bag? Can we really funnel everything in that bag into a decision by a tribunal of strangers that what occurred more than two decades ago was holy or unholy?

Some marriages work and some do not. Some marriages that once soared heavenward fall to Earth, because the people in them fail, as humans are wont to do. Some marriages that are devoid of intimacy and would qualify for annulment by acclamation if they were ever put on trial inexplicably endure, yet the church does not shun such couples because they continue to live together in "unholy" matrimony. These variations are not explained by a miscarriage of grace at the time these unions were conceived. They are simply an expression of the human condition.

I am no theologian, but I do take to heart the advice of St. Paul to "test everything, and hold fast to what is good" (1 Thess. 5: 21). I tested these questions for years, and I could never reconcile the Christ who offered living water at Jacob's Well to a woman with five husbands (John 4:18) with the church that was now offering me a choice between a show trial and a life of abject loneliness. Of all the qualities that describe Christ's life and mission on Earth, legalism and a preference for form over substance are not among them.

On this night at sea, in the sixty miles that separate Beaufort and Masonboro Inlet, I pondered these questions again as I had many times before and came to the same conclusion: I believe that the blood of Christ is sufficient to atone not just for some of our weaknesses and failures, but for all of them, and that the mercy of Christ is sufficient to allow us—all of us—to try again when we fail to imitate Him.

Chapter 14

A Voice in the Darkness

I arrived off Masonboro Inlet on the morning of Thanksgiving Day, happy to be alive and marveling again at how the slow accretion of wind and time can move an 11,700-pound vessel such a distance so easily. I was anxious to make the docks at Southport, some twenty-five miles away, because of the difficulty in navigating the shallows of Snow's Cut in the Intracoastal Waterway at night.

One has to go through the waterway on the route from Masonboro Inlet to Southport to avoid Frying Pan Shoals off Bald Head Island. Bald Head is the thorn-shaped southeastern tip of North Carolina that juts out into the Atlantic. The seas heap up here where the ocean rises from deep water onto the shoals.

The shoals extend far out to sea, near the western edge of the Gulf Stream. To sail south, offshore, and get safely around them, you would have to enter the Gulf Stream and fight your way against a current pushing north at three knots. It is easier and safer to motor the shorter distance down the Intracoastal Waterway and come out at Southport, where the offshore route all the way to Florida is deep water well west of the stream.

I had made the inland passage through Snow's Cut a half dozen times at night by necessity. Each one was as nerve-wracking as the last, but one in particular stood out in my memory.

It was January 2007, and three men had sailed with me to take the *Gypsy Moon* from New Bern to Bald Head Island. After a windless night on the offshore run from Beaufort, a brisk southwest breeze arrived at midmorning off Masonboro Inlet, and we could not resist riding it well offshore, just to let the boat stretch her legs. That worthwhile diversion cost us daylight, however, and we found ourselves crawling through Snow's Cut after dark.

The cut is wide and deep where it passes under the highway bridge, but farther south, in the Cape Fear River, the distances between markers in the channel grow longer, and the water outside the channel shoals to inches thin. To avoid running aground, I had one man on the bow using a spotlight to find the next channel marker, one man on the helm, and one man below, calling out depths from the chart. I was watching the depth sounder and the three of them. The helmsman was following a compass course based on the chart when depth soundings that had been steadily above twenty-two feet started to fall. The boat needed close to five feet of water to float. The channel depth was not uniform, though, and there were some places within the channel proper that had shoaled. It was not immediately clear that we were off course.

As the number on the depth sounder continued to drop and passed sixteen, I asked the chart man what our depth should be at that part of the channel. "Twenty-two," he shouted back. Fearing we were only a few seconds away from knee-deep mud, I grabbed the wheel from the helmsman and whirled the boat around 180 degrees to retrace the course over which we had just come, back to safe water. At that moment, a calm voice clearly spoke over channel 16 on the ship's radio.

The voice was addressing the crew of a boat heading through Snow's Cut between markers that he numbered correctly, for our location, and he called for us to answer. He did not identify himself or ask us, as the coast guard would certainly do, to switch to a working channel. He simply instructed us what compass course to steer from our present location to return to the channel, and where to steer from there. His instructions were dead-on.

When he signed off without further ado, I looked around the water, expecting to spot a shrimper or a workboat at anchor within visual range whose skipper had observed our error and called us on the radio to put us back on our way. The hair on the back of my neck stood up when I realized there was no one on the water that night but us.

I called for the man on the radio to thank him for his assistance, but no one answered. I looked again, far out into the river that leads into Wilmington, and, again, saw not a soul.

The coast guard trains all its radiomen in the same seamanlike elocution. They will hail only—never talk—on channel 16 before insisting that you switch to a working channel, 22 Alpha. This fellow was not coast guard, nor was he anywhere to be seen. We never heard from him again.

As time went by, I surmised that the events of September 11, 2001, had brought many unseen changes to our nation's borders, including the need to know who and what is riding around our coastlines. Perhaps nowhere was the need for these changes more acutely felt than close to Southport, next door to the Shearon Harris Nuclear Power Plant. I could be wrong about that. What I do know is that the lone wolf who helped us that night had some awfully big eyes, the better to see us with.

Chapter 15

THANKSGIVING

On that blessedly fair Thanksgiving Day in 2009, I made good time coming down the waterway and was well past Snow's Cut, nearly to the docks at Southport Marina, when the light started to fade. I arrived there after hours, tired and feeling more than a little sorry for myself for being alone on this sand spit of the Carolina coast with nothing much to eat on Thanksgiving.

The marina staff had all gone home, so I brought the *Gypsy Moon* alongside the fuel dock. I planned to spend the night there and get my regular slip assignment in the morning. No sooner had I landed than I had to rodeo the boat around to a new location, because the space close to the fuel pumps had no electrical power—a fire precaution. Finally, I got the old girl all tucked in among some pretty fancy company, including a rather large and well-loved cabin cruiser directly abeam. It felt odd that my boat was no longer moving, as I certainly still was.

After shaking off as much of the sea as I cared to, I set about the doleful task of inspecting the candidates for Thanksgiving dinner from the ship's larder. A lovely can of Chef Boyardee Ravioli won the prize. With opener in hand, I was just about to do the honors when a knock came on the hull.

I stepped outside and saw a woman standing on the dock beside my port lifelines. She asked me if I would care to have some of the Thanksgiving dinner she had prepared for herself and her husband aboard the shiny cabin cruiser next to me. More than a little astonished and wondering whether she might be the vanguard of an intervention team, I managed an enthusiastic acceptance. I returned Monsieur Boyardee safely to his locker, and my serendipitous host returned with a steaming plate of sliced turkey, homemade gravy, cranberry sauce, green bean casserole, mashed potatoes, dinner rolls, and a side of pumpkin pie. Had I not saved one hand for the ship, I likely would have fallen overboard in my amazement.

The woman on the dock grinned at my excitement. I insisted that she let me snap her picture with plate in hand, and she snapped one of me with the unopened can of ravioli. She and her husband were retired and cruising the waterway between Georgia and New Jersey. She asked me where I was bound. When I said the words "Nassau" and "solo," I got the by-then expected reaction of admiration mixed with envy and concern. In truth, though, I was the envious one.

The woman left me to my feast. I knew she would be returning to a well-fed and well-loved man who would share with her across a pillow, that night, the details of the day—including the story of the strange ravioli lover on the boat next door—as they drifted off to sleep together. I wanted that. I wanted that more than the meal I was starving to eat. I wanted that more than anything.

Late that night, after dishes had been returned with profuse thanks to my hosts, I opened my laptop and went online. I had a mission in mind.

It had been almost a year and a half since I'd ventured into the online dating world. My earlier travels in this strange land of ritualized head-hunting had run mostly in circles, but the road I was on was clearly a bridge to nowhere. My profile wistfully described a "sailor seeking pearl." I paused awhile to consider whether I really wanted to take this journey in addition to the one I had just begun, but the answer had already come to me in the middle of a delicious meal. For my safe passage, for that meal, and for all that it signified to me, I truly gave thanks. Then I hit the button marked "send" and lay down for a deep and dreamless sleep.

LATITUDE 32.77.90 N

LONGITUDE 79.95.15 W

CHARLESTON, SOUTH CAROLINA

Chapter 16

A COLD RAIN

What I have so long disliked about being a Yankee sailor is the cold. Not just the cold, but the cloying frigidity of cold air mixed with the mist and rain of brooding, sunless days. I shudder as I write these words. Lo these many years I have spent in the South, yet I have not escaped it. Well do I recall winter mornings even on the gulf coast of Texas that warranted every stitch of my wool socks and every inch of my leather boots—the same armor I once wore atop leafless Tennessee hills in pursuit of phantom deer. (The deer were much warmer than I, and therefore content to wait in stillness, unseen, until the oddly shivering archer departed their woods for easier quarry at the nearest hamburger stand.) Ever thus has been the source of my attraction to distant tropic islands. Ever thus has been my longing and my aim.

The cold is worse for sailors, because the lower temperatures cling to water and linger there well after the rest of nature has given up the grudge of winter. Yet a man's addiction to boats and the sea usually cannot abide the slow arrival of spring, and so the hapless sailor returns to open the shuttered cabin of his sleeping vessel and ask her again to dance, to relieve his wintering despair. When he does so and leads her out onto the steps of a chilled morning, in a harbor empty of other vessels, the scene unfolds with all the awkwardness of a couple arriving at a party that no one else has chosen to attend. Still, the dance goes on, however briefly and regrettably in the freezing rain, until the captain—his haste by then to all apparent—leads his ever-willing partner back to her berth to await a warmer afternoon.

So was the scene in December 2009 when I arrived at the marina in Southport, North Carolina, with the intention of departing for the open sea. It was, naturally, a gray day with a fresh breeze a bit too cool for comfort. The sky seemed low enough to touch and filled with what would surely become a lingering rain. It was, in other words, another signature beginning in the logbook of the *Gypsy Moon*.

As usual, more than a few logistical contortions preceded my departure. A recalcitrant opposing counsel, renewing for a fourth and unsuccessful time a motion to compel the production of some privileged and impertinent document, had scheduled a hearing with the minimum of notice, requiring a postponement of the voyage. I arrived at the courthouse to argue the point, then continued to the nearest telephone booth for a costume change from corporate lawyer to vagabond sailor. Once matters were finally in order, I came by rented car to Southport with plans to leave aboard the *Gypsy Moon*, bound for Nassau.

Chapter 17

A Simple Vessel

There is a by-now familiar dynamic in my conversations with strangers onshore while preparing to leave on a voyage. A sailor planning to go somewhere beyond the outer channel marker is easy to spot amid the general lethargy of life in a marina, so questions inevitably arise about where he is bound. When the answer entails a long voyage on the open ocean, in the listener's eyes I see quick flashes of worry as images of disaster flicker in the imagination. Such concerns are often obliquely expressed for fear of giving offense. To my stated intention to take the *Gypsy Moon* to sea on her first voyage to the Bahamas, in 2007, one dockmaster's only reply was, "In that boat?"

To be fair, the *Gypsy Moon*'s length, at 32 feet 4 inches overall, has become something of an anomaly among oceangoing vessels in the same way that the 5-foot 10-inch, 165-pound halfback has become an anomaly in professional football. It's not that the average man can't play the game well. It's just that fans are more entertained by seeing the game played by men twice his size.

It was not always so. In an old photo album I have the picture of an old girlfriend standing at the rail of the harbor ferry in Annapolis in 1975. Behind her one can clearly see an assortment of boats in the harbor. The girl having long been forgotten, the first thing I notice in looking at that picture is the wide array of sailboats moored in the same place where today you would find a great predominance of powerboats—further proof, as if any were needed, of the continued general trundling along of things to hell in a handbasket. The second thing I notice is that the largest of the sailboats in the picture appears to be about twenty-eight feet long, among many smaller vessels. Today, most boatbuilders don't make a sailboat smaller than forty feet long. Americans' taste in boats has changed in ways no different than their taste in homes, which have tripled in average size since the 1950s, just as the size of the average American family has shrunk by similar proportions.

Yet there are naysayers to every trend, and I am happily among those who still sing the virtues of the simpler, smaller boat. Two of my heroes are Lin and Larry Pardey, famous for their many round-the-world voyages aboard engineless sailboats smaller than thirty feet long overall. I had occasion to step aboard their twenty-eight-foot cutter, *Serrafyn*, when she was on display one year at the Annapolis boat show. Her head (toilet) was a simple manual system that the Pardeys indelicately described as "bucket and chuck it." With no engine, she had sailed around the world—twice. In tight harbors where sailing was impractical or when winds were light, the Pardeys used a single long oar passed through chocks on the stern railing to scull the boat forward.

Like *Serrafyn*, the *Gypsy Moon* will never spend a day in port waiting for the arrival of a new watermaker pump, radar scanner, single-sideband transceiver, generator valve spring, electric-winch motor, or new ideas on how to make a refrigeration system three degrees cooler than lukewarm. She is outfitted with none of these extravagances. She is free not only from their cost and complication, but also from slavery to their insatiable demand for fuel and engine-driven battery power. She is a simple boat, commanded by a simple (if not simpleminded) captain.

The boatyards and marine supply stores in the United States are filled to the rafters on most Saturdays with wannabe naval engineers of every stripe, secretly delighted that a faulty macerator pump or corroded water heater will consign them to the deepest recesses of the bilge for the duration of the weekend. I have always made a point of waving at these men in polite encouragement as my little boat sputters out of the marina on the way to go sailing.

There are economic advantages to a boat not merely simpler but smaller than today's normative forty-five- or fifty-footer. For every foot of increase in a boat's length, the expenses associated with maintaining and rigging the vessel become exponentially greater. A longer boat needs a taller mast with bigger sails and heavier rigging—all at a disproportionately greater cost. The thirty-six-footer that cannot fit into her owner's old thirty-foot slip must take another slip in the marina in the next available size—usually forty or fifty feet, for thousands of dollars more per year. The prices of haul-outs, bottom paint, cleaning, storage, insurance, and hull repairs all rise dramatically with even modest increases in boat length. When J. P. Morgan famously said that anyone who had to ask how much it costs to own a boat couldn't afford one, he was standing beside his 302-foot steamer *Corsair*, not a humble vessel the likes of *Gypsy Moon*.

There are practical advantages to the sailboat of moderate length, as well. One man can sail her alone or with a wife appointed only to the task of calling for a taxi should he drop dead, whereas the skipper of a well-found fifty-foot beauty is forever trolling the neighborhood for crew, pleading for able-bodied men as the English navy once did in the press-gangs of yore, only without the threat of violence. Those who join him he will entertain lavishly in exchange for their help in tiptoeing his expensive baby, like a nervous elephant, out of her slip. When the afternoon thunderstorm arrives, his startled crew will be sent aloft to attack and wrestle the enormous, flogging tarpaulin of a mainsail onto a slippery, pitching deck. Having thus traumatized his friends, he will try with increasing difficulty to replenish their numbers on later voyages, until at last his well of goodwill runs dry. When that day arrives, his beauty will retire beside her enormous kin at the marina until the barnacles or the boat brokers overtake her and she is delivered happily to some other unwitting would-be Lord Nelson. From this cycle in most sailors' lives comes the adage that owning a boat is like standing in a raincoat in a cold shower and tearing up hundred-dollar bills. The smart ones get out and dry off when they're tearing up twenties.

But I digress. All of this serves only to explain why I bristled when a dockhand at Southport Marina reacted with a whiff of astonishment upon hearing my plan to sail the *Gypsy Moon* offshore, nonstop, to Nassau. I felt that he was slighting my boat as she lay alongside the rows of enormous stay-at-homes sleeping in their slips, although he likely intended no such thing. In truth, the dockhand's raised eyebrows were all the more irritating because they reflected my own unspoken doubts.

I knew, on that fourth of December 2009, when I stood on deck readying sails and running through my checklist to take the *Gypsy Moon* to sea, that I would make good on my intention to set sail. I knew that with the same certainty that the Little Leaguer knows, when his name is called, that his feet will trudge to the batter's box, even as he doubts with equal fervor that his swing will ever meet the ball.

I honestly didn't think I'd make it all the way to Nassau. For whatever reason, I had allowed Nassau to become in my imagination, with each passing day, a destination of Homeric proportions.

Before I left, my pastor had given me a book as cargo. The book told the history of the old stone cathedral of Christ Church in Raleigh. I was charged with the task of presenting it as a gift to the pastor of Christ Church in Nassau, whose steeple was raised in 1830. Though I didn't know it then, my voyage would be an occasion for some to wonder whether I ought to have enlisted a few good Baptists to pray for me along with the Episcopalians.

Chapter 18

A FOLLOWING SEA

The mouth of the Cape Fear River is a wide, forlorn, and feature-less place where the land of North Carolina points its southeastern-most end to the sea. A few well-to-do residents, tired service work-ers, and returning vacationers taking the private ferry to Southport from Bald Head Island looked with passing interest at the thirty-two-foot sloop making her way, alone, toward the open ocean. The sky and sea were a continuous pale gray. Here, in a deep shipping channel that requires constant vigilance against shoaling from swift, swirling tides, great ocean freighters come and go.

There is a feeling of desolation to the waters around Southport that holds no welcome. No brightly colored little sloops filled with laughing children dither back and forth among the sandbars there. People and ships pass through these roads quickly and with deter-mination to be somewhere else. It is a place between places—like a graveyard in the evening—that urges one not to linger. I, too, was eager to be away. I hurried along until I could look back and see the sweep of the Oak Island Light in my wake. I was at sea at last, again.

I passed through a gentle chop at 1700 hours on my way to the outer channel marker and took a bearing on Frying Pan Shoals, to stay well off. I was headed 197 degrees magnetic, just west of due south. Flying at first only a working jib to starboard and then only her main, the *Gypsy Moon* hiked up her skirt, put her shoulder down, and ran at six knots on a broad reach. This point of sail is where she finds her heart. With the wind whipping at her heels, she pulls like an old racehorse who hasn't forgotten the thrill of the chase, even if she can't match the younger fillies for speed.

As night set in, a light rain began to fall, and I headed for the shelter of the cabin. I was still on the uphill slope of the learning curve on how to use the Monitor self-steering wind vane, which in the early stages of the voyage had been only so much ornamental steel hanging off the stern. Once I understood the rather mysterious incantations of line tension, vane direction, and sail trim necessary to make the thing work, it proved itself an amazing device capable of sailing the boat on a straight and steady course for days on end without my bothersome interference at the helm. What the Monitor clearly could not do, however, was steer a straight course dead downwind. And in the norther blowing that day off Southport, dead downwind was where I needed to go.

The electronic autopilot, which gobbles power but respects neither the speed nor the direction of the wind, was my only respite from an unending rain-soaked vigil at the helm to keep the boat on course. So, with the sail nicely trimmed and tight, I set the autopilot to the compass course dead off the wind and went below to enjoy the wonderful peace of a warm cabin in a boat moving well at sea.

It was a short-lived peace. As I sailed through the night under the stoic guidance of the autopilot, running from gusty weather and rain, the waves rose to about four feet high. The stern would ride up the front and slide down the back of each successive roller, and the autopilot would fight against the boat's instinctive wish to turn and face the wind. As the wind strengthened, so did the forces bearing on the autopilot, which groaned and creaked and clattered from its effort to get the *Gypsy Moon* to the church on time.

By late afternoon on the second day, the log recorded "high winds, rough seas near Charleston, 28 miles northeast." It was time for a sail change. I'd known I was doing the "safe" thing when, during the preceding summer in Annapolis, I had arranged for a sailmaker to cut and sew a storm trysail and for a rigger to rivet a stainless steel external track to the mast on which to hoist it, but I never thought I'd need the thing. It's very old-school. Only one boat in a hundred carries a storm trysail nowadays. I felt good about having one, but in truth, I thought I'd have about as much use for it on the open sea as I would a bomb shelter. Wrong again.

When the waves rose to five feet, I mustered the storm trysail on the cabin top and tried to recall exactly which end went where, as the stiff, thick new sail spilled from its bag and scudded along the wet decks. Up in its tracks along the mast it went, pulled by the main halyard, until it snapped open in the freshening breeze with a loud *craa-ack* and came to a disorderly salute. Though only one-third the area of the mainsail, when caught by the wind the trysail violently jerked its outhaul line, which I held tightly in my hand. I discovered that I lacked the strength to tie it off. I had forgotten to rig a block and tackle to use in making the line fast, but I could not simply let go of the reins of this wild mustang and let her run.

After standing there stupidly for a moment, with my arm jerking back and forth in the air like a conductor's baton in the 1812 Overture, I formed a plan. I made my way to the cockpit, ran the line once through a wire bail on the end of the boom, and ran the free end back through the grommet on the clew of the sail, then back through the bail on the boom. With this, I immediately had more authority over the situation. Shortening the line, I pulled the flailing canvas until it was tight and all was suddenly quiet. With her sail area thus reduced, the boat's motion slowed and eased. However, the clatter and clacking of the gears in the autopilot continued unabated as it strove against the pressure of the waves on the rudder to keep the boat and her crew on a straight and narrow path.

Chapter 19

A Yearning

There was a yearning that followed me to sea and was my constant companion on bright, idle days and long night watches. Alone though I was, I was always accompanied by my thoughts: assorted hopes, fears, and regrets. They rolled on in an endless stream in my mind along with the sound of the ocean.

Inches from where I laid my head to sleep, the water coursing across the outside of the hull sounded like a babbling brook as it rushed to become a part of my past. I cherished the memory of it. I suspect we would all better use and savor our time on Earth if we could sense each moment of our lives slipping astern with the same constancy and clarity as a sailor knows the passing of his ship's wake.

The thoughts of those idle hours turned always to another. I knew not who she was or even who she might be, but I yearned for her with an ache that had lingered for decades. I have learned to ask God for my longings, however disinclined He might be to grant them. And so I prayed to God as I had so often before for that prize that neither effort nor merit nor money nor my compulsion for planning and organization could attain. I wanted the Big One. With heaven yet beyond my grasp, I wanted what on Earth would be its closest foretaste. I prayed that God would help me find a good woman with whom to share my life. I remember the very moment and the supine posture from which this prayer was lifted heavenward. It would be the first of two petitions on this passage.

We are all wounded and alone in some way, but the ebb and flow of daily life in cities and towns filled with people has an anesthetic effect. There is no greater sense of being truly, completely alone than what is to be found in a small boat far out at sea. It clears the mind. It places a man apart from everything and everyone and gives him a profound sense of his own smallness, though not a sense of insignificance. Away from the neon and the rush, far from Walmart, out of earshot of the chattering of pundits and politicians, eventually there is only God. When God is your only companion, either there is an awkward silence or there is prayer.

American pop culture has long celebrated the steely-eyed loner who does not pray but, rather, stoically endures life's hardships. He is ever the hero of song and the silver screen. I have never found him in my own character, but I put my young son to sleep each night for many years to the tune of "Desperado." Sung and played however feebly on my guitar, the words of this song still rang true: "Come down from your fences... and let somebody love you, before it's too late." When I began this voyage, I had been trying to come down from those fences and find someone for so long that it seemed I might be destined to become the drifter pitied in that song.

But yearning that becomes desperation is a dangerous thing. Desperation is the father of many orphans. With no small difficulty I had learned to choose patience and deliberation over desperation in my own life, after my divorce, as I began to pursue the dream of finding a true partner and friend. That, too, was a journey.

Along that pilgrim road, I had to learn to cut away stagnant, static, and sometimes toxic relationships, eventually acquiring some considerable skill with the blade from frequent and dispassionate use. I learned to say "no thanks," "not yet," "no more," "good-bye," and "good riddance" and to value my innermost desire over concern for someone else's disappointment. In time, a trail of bruised and broken hearts—my own among them—lay in my wake. But no one can live long by that sword.

To avoid becoming submerged in my solitude and to find some greater purpose for my voyage (or perhaps it might be fairly said merely to appear to do so), months earlier I had written to the rector of Christ Church in Nassau to propose that when I sailed into his harbor (triumphant and covered in glory, I must have seemed absurdly to suggest), I would be pleased to be employed in some needed manual labor to benefit the church. I received no reply, I am not surprised to say. Bahamians are not aborigines in need of my beneficence. But I was undeterred at the time. This small mission, though it would go unfulfilled, gave me a brighter star to follow.

Chapter 20

AFRICA BECKONS

The wind was rising. The temperature was also falling, even as the *Gypsy Moon* forged her way farther down the coast of South Carolina. The night sky was spitting a cold, uncomfortable, and occasional rain. The drops flew in like random sniper fire from some unseen assassin hiding in the darkness above. The electronic autopilot continued its loud lamentations as it kept the rudder braced against an unruly following sea.

It was late in the evening when I finally saw the sea buoy marking the entrance to the Fort Sumter Range. With the task of keeping sure footing in the cabin getting harder as the boat pitched and rolled, I had not bothered to chart the hour in the log. But I knew I was making good time—the northerly breeze had seen to that, scudding me along at a constant pace with the following waves pushing me faster still. Southport was now nearly 130 miles to the north. The *Gypsy Moon* had stretched her legs and run once again like a teenager in love.

Fort Sumter Range is the name of the channel leading into Charleston. Big ships line up far out at sea on a straight line leading to two lighted range markers—a shorter one in front and a taller one behind—erected onshore. The markers serve the same purpose as the sights on a rifle. When the lights of the range markers line up, the helmsman can be assured that his vessel is aimed down the deep middle of the channel. The helmsman's task is then to keep the two range markers perpendicular in his sights as he shoots his vessel shoreward, like a bullet through a barrel. If the lower range marker appears to move to starboard below the upper marker, he knows the ship is drifting off course into shallow water to port, and vice versa.

I was seventeen miles out on the range from Fort Sumter at the point where I crossed the channel, heading south. Seeing the flashing light of the sea buoy passing so close abeam was a faintly startling reminder of the Hand of Man that I had left behind seemingly long ago, although in reality it was only the day before. I looked down the range as I crossed it on a perpendicular course and saw the lights of the channel markers line up like an airport runway. That was a path to safety and comfort, I knew. Although I was as safe as a babe in his cradle out on the open ocean, I was also at that moment as uncomfortable as one in a wet diaper long overdue for changing.

But to be warm and ashore in Charleston was not the mission I had undertaken back on the Magothy River in August. There was nothing stopping me, and I would not stop. The boat held her course. The waves and wind, though a bit too rough for comfort, were merely a spate of winter weather and not a storm at all. With renewed resolve, I watched Charleston fade astern and looked over the chart for the course ahead.

Below Charleston, the continental United States begins the gradual eastward sweep that brings the coastline and the western wall of the Gulf Stream ever closer, until in Florida the stream flows as close as a mile offshore. The Gulf Stream, which runs from south to north, is the mortal enemy of any wind that blows from north to south. Where the two converge they do terrible battle, kicking up steep and confused seas. A man on a small boat should no more want to sail through the middle of such a contest than to try to separate two warring cats. I certainly wanted no part of this altercation, which, I was well aware, was taking place some thirty miles to the east.

With no crew other than my own two hands to help me remain on a southerly course, I was dependent on the herculean efforts of my electronic autopilot. The wind vane is a marvelous device with a single limitation: it cannot with any effectiveness keep a vessel on a due-south heading in a north wind with following seas. Only an electronic mind that knows its heading (and has a gear ratio strong enough to hold it) can do that job. So far, the wheel autopilot had been whirring, clacking, and grinding at that task in the cold rain with greater determination than I could have summoned from myself or any human helmsman.

I lay down for a few winks of sleep as the ship settled in for the long slog. Not long after I had closed my eyes, I heard the sound of breaking plastic and stripping gears as the electronic autopilot entered its death throes. The machine had yielded at last to the relentless power of nature. Control of the helm was lost. The robotic arm of the autopilot frantically whirred its warning that the boat was off course, but that warning now went unheeded. I jumped up and ran out on deck.

As soon as her electronic taskmaster had breathed his last, the *Gypsy Moon* followed her heart's desire to turn and face the weather. She was now headed northeast, shoulder down and hard on the wind on what would have been a wonderful course for Ireland, had it been my intention to visit the Auld Sod.

Out in the open cockpit, the chilling rain and blustery wind that had been a mere spectacle from the vantage point of a dry cabin were now a considerable annoyance to me as I made preparations to implement Plan B. I would deploy the Monitor Windvane, I decided, on a mission to do something as close as possible to what it could not, which was to sail due south. Setting the vane for a course just east of south, I adjusted the lines and hoped for the best. When the boat finally kept a manageable heading to the southeast, my spirits rose.

I could zig south by southeast for several miles, I thought, until I felt the whips and lashes of the Gulf Stream, at which point I could zag back west toward the calmer waters of the coast. But ere that thought was through, the boat overcame the correction of the vane and began backsliding into her old vices. She was now offering to compromise on a due-easterly heading in response to my demand that she head south, pleading like an insolent teenager that I should let her go to Africa if not to Ireland. This would not do.

Again and again I tinkered with rudder line tension, vane angle, sail trim, and supplications to the self-steering gods as I sat in the tossing, rain-slicked cockpit, miles south of Charleston, well offshore, loosely draped in a leaking ten-dollar raincoat that was more symbolic than actual shelter against the elements.

Finally, the vane held the boat on a southeasterly course for more than a few moments. I waited expectantly for her to veer off again, but she did not. It appeared that I had found that magic "groove" in which sails, hull, and rudder work in a cacophony of cross-purposes that drive the vessel in a single intended direction. Contented with this effort and congratulating myself for not giving in to the weather gods, I retired again to the warmth and shelter of the cabin against the cold night.

I was exhausted. Sleep, when it does come in periods of rough weather, is fitful at best. As I lay down to rest that night in the belly of the whale that was my little ship, I became accustomed, as I usually do, to the motion of the boat on her heading. Lying prone in the six-foot four-inch pilot berth that runs along the port side on the ship's stern quarter, I was below the waterline. My body rose and fell and swayed from side to side—more gently because I was low in the ship's center of gravity—in unison with the hull moving through the waves. On this broad reach, with the wind coming over her port quarter and her sails set to starboard, the ship plunged forward with a regularity that recalled the nodding head of a child's rocking horse. By the repetition of this motion I was lulled once again to sleep. Two hours later, by the unmistakable interruption of that motion, I was shaken rudely awake.

It was sometime near four in the morning, I can only guess. I had long since abandoned the niceties of log-keeping in these troublesome hours. I awoke to find that the wind and seas had risen a notch higher. Together these forces had broken the will of the self-steering vane, and the *Gypsy Moon* had returned to an easterly imperative. It was Africa or nothing, my headstrong ship was telling me. There would be no southerly heading that night.

I was not prepared for a fistfight with the Gulf Stream, where I was clearly headed. Nor would such a contest have been to any purpose, for I would only be stopped still by that current, if not carried slowly backward to the place from whence I had come. Time and again, I tinkered with the wind vane, collapsing for a while in the pilot berth until the flapping of sails and increasing angle of heel signaled the ship's renewed objection to my command.

This battle of wills continued until dawn, when I finally hove to the boat under a gray sky. Taking my position, I saw that I had come some twenty miles south of Charleston. I knew I had to return there to seek shelter, and a wave of regret overcame me that I had not turned back many miles earlier, when the autopilot had first failed.

I remember the feeling of defeat in that moment. I had no delusions of grandeur or heroic fate, but I had harbored the private conceit that my voyage in some small way enjoyed the protection of God's providence and mercy. It seemed contrary to His plans and mine that I should be foiled in my effort to reach Nassau, headed as I was on a mission of charity to the church there. Perhaps in that regard God had taken my altruistic intentions no more seriously than I had taken them myself.

Who, after all, was I really fooling? I had only to look in the mirror to see a spoiled, self-involved, middle-aged man in the throes of a midlife crisis, running from an adulterous affair, a failed marriage, and a failed career. But I could also look in the mirror and see a hopeful eleven-year-old boy, finally realizing after forty years the dream of that day when an unbroken horizon would meet a stalwart ship and a man with the freedom and the will to take her there. I did not judge the man or the boy, and I prayed that God would not judge either.

In that hour I prayed, too, in a way that I had not before. Lying in my bunk, stymied in my efforts and feeling quite annoyed with the whole situation, I lifted to the heavens a prayer of a single word: "Why?" It was the second petition of that passage.

I knew not to wait out there on the open ocean for an answer. God sometimes seems in no more of a hurry to read my letters to Him than I am to read His letters to me. But as St. Paul teaches, we see the contours of God's plans now only as through a glass, darkly. What my eyes could not see, and what I did not know, was that my prayers had a single answer, and that answer was already at hand.

Chapter 21

A Harbor Homecoming

Charleston is a harbor well familiar to me. I had gone there in 2003 to acquire the *Gypsy Moon* from her former owner. Her name then was *Moonlighter,* formerly *The Gypsy in Me.* In a nod to seagoing superstition against renaming boats, I incorporated both names into *Gypsy Moon.* Neptune, so far as I can tell, has been pleased.

I had intentionally come back to Charleston once before, in 2007, when the *Gypsy Moon* was en route to the Bahamas with a crew of four men. In that more modest undertaking, I had arranged to sail to the Abaco Islands in a series of 120-mile legs over six weekends, coastwise down the Eastern Seaboard, with each leg manned by enough crew to keep a twenty-four-hour watch. However loftier my ambitions had been for this second expedition to be nonstop, it appeared that I was following much the same herky-jerky heading as before, only without the crew.

It was a bracing upwind sail for the twenty miles back to the channel at Charleston. Had I been headed to the open sea it would have been thrilling, but knowing that my destination was a marina and an admission of defeat, the voyage had all the excitement of a cab ride. In the interminable hours it took me to fetch the Fort Sumter Range again, I came to appreciate just how far and long my battle with the wind vane the previous night had gone on.

By midday I was finally in the channel, and the *Gypsy Moon's* two-cylinder diesel engine rumbled once more to life in the shadow of a large container ship coming to port beside her. It is a long, tedious way through the Fort Sumter Range, and the absence of any significant hazard to navigation for all but the most foolhardy makes for mind-numbing boredom on a slow-going sailboat under power. My mind was already miles away and busy with plans for my return to Raleigh when boredom was banished. The engine transmission suddenly refused to answer, and I could make no way.

I let the helm fly free and ran up on the cabin top to raise the sails. The *Gypsy Moon*, now leaderless, dodged and veered of her own accord across the channel. Finally catching the wind and the ability to steer, I maneuvered into a protected anchorage amid the shallows and dropped anchor with sails still flying. The plough dug into the sand and snubbed up the anchor rode smartly in the bow chocks, whipping my little boat around to attention like a mother grabbing a wayward child by the nose. I lay there in the shadows of Fort Sumter, where the first shots of the Civil War were fired, and wondered who, exactly, had decided to shoot out both my autopilot and my engine transmission on this voyage. There would be no leaving Charleston anytime soon, while repairs were made.

A likable towboat captain (they are uniformly likable fellows, I have found) was quickly on the scene. He threw me a bridle to pull the *Gypsy Moon* against the swift tide that flows in the Ashley River up to Charleston City Marina, where I had first made my boat's acquaintance nearly seven years before.

The Charleston City Marina is staffed by platoons of mannerly and officious southern boys in starched uniforms who no doubt come from what in an earlier day might have been called the "better families." They gave no appearance in the least of needing my business or my money, but they required a considerable sum of the latter for the privilege of taking on the *Gypsy Moon* until repairs could be completed.

I spent the next four hours maneuvering a wheelbarrow up and down the ramps of the marina, offloading a mountain of supplies and provisions from the *Gypsy Moon* into a rented compact car. I wasn't altogether sure how extensive the needed engine repairs would be or whether I could afford them. I was also, in my heart of hearts, less enamored of the idea of continuing the voyage than I had been two days earlier. What had once seemed so exciting and adventurous in the telling was turning out to be damned lonely and expensive in the doing. Feverish thoughts again came of selling the boat. I knew that would be rash, but I decided to strip her of anything of added value before I drove back to Raleigh. I wanted to be ready to let her go, if it came to that.

This experience of remorse and others like it, as the voyage continued, taught me something about myself. I know that I come too quickly to these overreactions of despair. I know but often fail to learn that I must give time and temperament their due. At that particular moment, I was greatly discouraged and more than a little embarrassed, frankly, that my once-grand adventure had come to naught. I didn't know it then, but that fog was about to clear.

Chapter 22

THE SIREN'S SONG

After returning to Raleigh, I received welcome news from the mechanic: my transmission problem was merely a parted cable that would be easily replaced, and the cost of a new drive unit on the autopilot would come in well south of my worst fears. The voyage was suddenly back on, my melancholy woes were just as quickly forgotten, and Nassau loomed even closer than it had before. With any luck, I thought, I'd be there by Christmas and just in time for Junkanoo—the Bahamian answer to Mardi Gras. I made plans to meet the boat on Friday, December 18, and set sail the following morning.

Not long after this happy news, another cheerful message came my way. It was a message of the most profound consequence for my life, though I surely didn't know it at the time. A woman named Susan, in South Carolina of all places, shared with me this intriguing prayer in an e-mail: "God, I wish I lived closer." It seemed then that God's in-box did runneth over.

She was responding to the online dating profile that I, carried away in a gush of hope and narcissism that spring eternal from the same well, had posted on Thanksgiving Day. On that day, after arriving alone again at another forlorn marina, I had resolved to cast my fate once more to the winds of the Internet. For all I knew and truly for all I had expected, my fate had been carried only briefly aloft on those winds before getting stuck in an unseen tree, there forever to remain. The early returns had not been promising. But this message from a lovely lady in South Carolina most certainly was.

Looking at her picture, what I noticed as soon as I recovered from the initial distraction of her impossibly long legs, rapturous hips, and flowing blond hair, and the careless typographical error concerning her age (only one year younger than I), was something about her face, and specifically her eyes. I don't mean her beauty, though beautiful she certainly is. It was something else. It was something new. It was something important.

The human mind, with its power to perceive the finest nuances of emotion, character, and intention in the face of another, is a wondrous thing. A child need only glance at his mother to know affection, approbation, or anxiety. What I saw in Susan's photograph that day eluded my powers of description, and for a while I remained unable to find words for it—even after I met her in person. I knew that I was seeing something very different from what I had seen in others, but I didn't know why or how that was so. I knew only that I wanted God to answer her prayer and mine, and I sensed that He already had. I wanted her to be closer, and I wanted to be closer to her.

Her address was listed as Ridgeville, South Carolina—a place unfamiliar to me. I knew it was nowhere near my home in Raleigh. I feared it might be far out of reach on the western end of the state, but I was delighted to learn that it was right outside Charleston, to which I planned very shortly to return. "What are the chances of that?" I thought.

We exchanged banal pleasantries and polite compliments by e-mail at first, as all participants in the modern Kabuki dance of online dating are obliged to do. I learned that she had skipped a grade in high school and graduated with a business degree from the College of Charleston a year earlier than I had stumbled out of the University of Maryland, skipping over no one. She had two teenagers and so did I, all spaced within four years of age. When I discovered that she had risen from payroll clerk to comptroller of a hospital before holding, for twenty-one years, her current position as director of accounting for Charleston's public works authority, I rejoiced that my radar for finding bitter, unemployed alimony mavens had malfunctioned at last.

Soon our correspondence crossed a kind of line. It became real. I noticed—or better to say I was astonished—that this woman was capable of the true intimacy of self-revelation. That is no small thing. We are all, to some degree, reluctant to allow others into our inner world. Women who have given their hearts to others, only to have them badly broken, are the most prone to this fear—the fear of getting close, of letting go, of being mocked, of being rejected, of being truly known, of surrendering control, of trusting men to catch them when they fall and risking that they won't. My sojourn through singlehood has been a fascinating study in human nature. Despite the recent discoveries concerning the planet Venus, I have met many women who are card-carrying citizens of Mars, some of whom are quite incapable of true intimacy. Their guard is up to stay.

There was something else about Susan, too. A capacity for intimacy is important, but it is not all we need to be lucky in love. Two people can be emotionally intimate yet want very different things in life. What I wanted and sorely needed was a partner, ready for marriage, who could commit to a life in which our relationship would be the first priority—the constant star around which the demands of our families, our careers, and every other aspect of our lives would find its orbit and fall into place. I made no apology because I refused to orbit some other star in some outer galaxy, and Susan expected no apology. She wanted the same thing. That was a first. Here, I thought, was not only a woman whom I could easily love and adore, but one who was capable of loving me back.

But we had to meet first.

I told her I was coming to Charleston on Friday, December 18, to spend the night aboard the boat in the marina and get ready to sail the next day. Following *The Boyfriend Handbook* to a tee, I proposed that we meet for coffee at a local shop near where she worked, in downtown Charleston. Coffee would be brief, giving both of us an easy out if the meeting didn't live up to our expectations.

Our expectations kept rising with each letter we shared, back and forth in the ether of e-mail. Soon the e-mail started coming with family photos attached. I marveled at my good fortune that she could actually be that gorgeous, a grown-up, and normal to boot. Coffee, it was quickly apparent, would hardly do. I had this one chance to impress her, and I needed more time. It would have to be dinner. She agreed.

Chapter 23

THE PROMISED LAND

It was not just raining but flooding in Charleston when I arrived for our date at the Peninsula Grill that Friday night. Recalling the winds that had crippled my ship and driven her ashore, and seeing the biblical rains that now threatened to bar my way back there, I began to suspect I might be starring unawares in some Cecil B. DeMille epic. Could a plague of locusts be far off?

Knowing that I would one day write this chapter, I have long wondered how I would find the words to describe the moment when I first met Susan. I can certainly report that a woman of remarkable beauty with a confident, winning smile and kind eyes strode into the foyer of the restaurant, wearing a black dress and carrying the world on a string. Those are the facts. But I must admit that beyond this, my skill for expositional narrative falls well short of the task. I can only hope that readers can give aid to my failing prose with the recollection of just such a moment in their own lives and know what I mean when I tell you that when I saw her, I *just knew.*

It is certainly true that not every first impression of mine has been authoritative, nor have all those decisions I have made quickly been wise. Prudence would have counseled more caution in coming to conclusions about my feelings for Susan, but my heart would hear nothing of it. I could have pretended after our first evening together that I didn't know she was *the one*, and she could have pretended the same thing about me. But had we been the kind of people for whom pretending came so easily, we would not have experienced such a powerful mutual attraction in the first place.

When I looked across the table at the face of the real woman smiling back at me over dinner, I noticed again that thing—that intangible something—that had caught my attention when I first looked at her photographs. For most of the evening, I struggled to put my finger on it, like the name of someone you think you might know but just can't recall. Then suddenly I realized what I was seeing. It was a face without guile.

There was no subterfuge and no artifice about this woman. She was not jaded or cynical or sarcastic. She was not gaming me. There was no come-hither stare, no intention to use her feminine charms to her clearly superior advantage. She was surrendered to the possibility that we might fall in love, with all its attendant dangers and complications and costs. Those were secondary or tertiary concerns for her. She wasn't afraid of that possibility or the risks it portended. She wasn't shrinking from the challenge before us. She wanted more than anything, it seemed, merely to be with me. I was defenseless against the honesty in her eyes.

I had been looking for these very qualities in a woman for so long, and my hope of their discovery had for so long been a mirage, that I did not have the capacity at first to understand that what I was seeing was real. Yet when the flicker of my understanding finally became a flame, it ignited my resolve with all the urgency of a five-alarm fire. I knew, in the course of an evening, that my life had been forever changed and that so, too, had hers.

Mr. DeMille had been characteristically busy, and so it was to be expected that an offshore gale followed the rain. Because of this weather I would be unable to leave the next day, which became the happy occasion for Susan's second invitation to dinner. This meal would be served on Saturday night aboard the *Gypsy Moon* by her captain. It was a camp-style affair brought forth from the ship's larder and prepared upon her antique alcohol stove. Canned chicken, diced tomatoes, onions, black beans, and garlic were sautéed in olive oil and served in a white sauce over pasta topped with grated Parmesan cheese, accompanied by candlelight, wine, and music for dancing in the two-by-two-foot space afforded by the cabin sole.

She brought family photo albums, we curled up in the vee berth together to go through them, and we both laughed at how everyone looked in the sixties. That was such a time of hopeful innocence. Examine the photographs of young families back then, and you can see it in their faces. It was a time when Martin Luther King, Jr., dreamed that we would all one day be free, and when John F. Kennedy called us to "bear the burden of a long twilight struggle" to see such dreams come true. But that burden proved too great for those men alone to bear, and an entire generation saw the shadows of that twilight struggle grow longer with their passing. We lost our innocence, and in some ways I think many of us from that generation have never regained that feeling of exuberant hope.

Looking across the table of my ship's salon at Susan, I had those feelings of hopefulness once more, and the innocence to believe that my hopes could come true. Kennedy needn't have worried about the Russians. Another American flew over the moon that night, and he made the trip without a rocket.

Chapter 24

The Pearl of Great Price

Sunday morning dawned over a strong breeze offshore at Charleston, with waves still running five to seven feet, according to the weatherman in my ship's radio. It was not certain at first that these conditions would continue into the afternoon, but as the day wore on and the wind did not abate, I knew that my departure would be delayed yet another day. That was all right by me.

I spent the better part of the day getting provisions squared away and the boat ready to sail. When I had done all I could do and it appeared that there was nothing left but to wait, I called Susan. She would be home that evening, and I was invited to come for dinner—our third together in as many days.

It was a big step. Single mothers are rightly cautious about introducing their children to any men they might be dating. Although Susan's children were not babies, at fifteen and seventeen they were still at an impressionable age. I would learn later that I was the only one in a long line of suitors who were accorded the honor of meeting them, but that did not surprise me in the least. Through words unspoken, I knew we shared the same plan. Things were moving fast.

That Sunday afternoon, I had written my innermost thoughts in a letter to give to Susan after dinner, knowing that I would be sailing the next day and at sea for perhaps a week after that, without the kind of constant communication that new love demands. I will spare you the seasickness that would surely overtake you were I to recite that purple prose. But I make no apologies to anyone for the way I felt then and still feel now. In those letters I spoke to Susan from the heart, and she gave me hers in return.

The next morning, I sailed out of Charleston Harbor a changed man living a changed life. I smile inside each time I recall hearing Susan's words through the fading signal on my cell phone as I worked the *Gypsy Moon* into the channel headed offshore on that bright Monday morning: "I am totally committed to you."

The die was cast. I was leaving to complete the voyage I had begun, but I had found at last the safe harbor that I knew would shelter both of us for the rest of our days. Eight months later, with the *Gypsy Moon* nodding at her lines in Nassau, we were married in the garden of our home in Raleigh. It was a simple ceremony conducted in the presence of our children, other family, and a small group of friends. As Susan spoke her vows, I saw again in her eyes that fearless surrender to love that I had discovered while waylaid in the harbor at Charleston. That was her gift to me. She was the Pearl of Great Price that I had searched so long and far to find. I pledged all that I have and all that I am to make her my own, and I will never let her go. I made that pledge in the words of a poem that I wrote for her as a wedding gift:

On Our Wedding Day
He sailed for Nassau, a man alone,
But a Siren's song he heard.
She called to him from Old Charles Town,
And his voyage was deterred.

The Pearl of Great Price

* * *

Hull and heart did find repair,
Where the lovely Siren sang.
Enraptured by her beauty, there,
He felt love's old sweet pang.

* * *

Hold fast now, lads. Let the rollers run.
Let the sea her treasures bear.
But of all the pearls beneath the waves,
There is none so fine or fair.

* * *

She takes her place, now, at his side,
On this, their wedding day.
The sea's brightest jewel is a blushing bride,
And the captain is come home to stay.

LATITUDE 28.40.88 N

LONGITUDE 80.62.73 W

PORT CANAVERAL, FLORIDA

Chapter 25

THE SECRET

It was December 21, 2009. I was sailing out of the harbor where I had just met the woman I believed I would someday marry. I didn't yet know but hoped she kindled the same flame. With Christmas only four days away, I was as giddy as old Ebenezer Scrooge in his moment of salvation. The dolphins that escorted me through the channel at Fort Sumter could have been sugarplum fairies, for all I cared or might have noticed on that heady morning.

The tide that swept me out of Charleston and back to the sea on a Monday in December had been a long time coming, but its sudden arrival was unexpected. To fix the latitude and longitude of my position in that moment and understand where I was headed from there, it is necessary to look back at the time and place where I first began.

I grew up in what is politely described in therapeutic circles nowadays as an "alcoholic family," which is an odd way of imagining a family. After all, a family doesn't take a drink—a man does, or, as F. Scott Fitzgerald more closely observed, the drink takes him. A man who drinks with purpose, not pleasure, is a lit fuse for whom booze is a powder keg. However slowly and quietly the fuse may burn, sooner or later any wives and children on the scene will be blasted skyward like so much cannon fodder, suspended awhile in a spectacular, wild flight from the pursuing laws of time and gravity.

Time and gravity always get their man.

Eventually, everyone who is elevated by the explosion falls back to Earth, scorched and smoldering, landing necessarily at the bottom of wherever they happen to be. When my dad hit bottom he kept rolling in a cloud of hot smoke, but the rest of us landed in Baltimore.

It was not long before that big bang when my mother, at the age of thirty-six, gave birth to me, her fourth and youngest child by ten years. She had no career and only a high school education. The year was 1958, and the women's movement was still a distant dream. Undaunted, she taught herself to type, took two jobs, and worked days, nights, and weekends. By the time I was eight, my brother and two sisters had left to make their way in the world. My mother moved the two of us from inner-city Baltimore to a one-bedroom apartment in the county that we could scarcely afford. The apartment was located next to Boys' Latin, a private prep school with a meandering campus on which I would come to trespass with impunity.

Baltimore, I discovered, is a "provincial" town. The word "province" describes a place that is defined more by its boundaries than its possibilities, more by what it excludes than what it welcomes. The boundaries in Baltimore in the sixties were ones of money, education, and social class, which were really just branches of the same tree. Baltimore then was exceedingly well organized along ethnic and socioeconomic lines, and cross-pollination was rare.

Growing up, I knew Baltimore—and specifically my neighborhood of Roland Park—as a place where an elite tribe wearing horn-rimmed tortoise shell glasses drove boxy forest-green Volvos with round headlights and tan leather seats so cracked and peeling that the sheepskins that covered them were clearly a thing of utility, not fashion. Their ancient axles creaked at every bend in the road like the timbers of an old ship. For every hundred thousand miles on the odometer, Nordic medallions were clamped to the front grille as proof that the owner's choice of something initially costlier and dowdier than his neighbor's Chevrolet, like his choice of investments and a wife, had been proven wiser with time. His neighbor likely had sent three Chevrolets to the junkyard in the same span of years, at greater total cost, while the quirky Volvo and its knowing owner soldiered steadily on.

I learned that no matter how elderly the member of this elite tribe, his trusted Volvo was tattooed with emblems readily identifying him to other tribesmen (and presumably protecting him from attack) as a member of a particular regional band, spelled out across the rear window in letters like Y-A-L-E or H-A-R-V-A-R-D or P-R-I-N-C-E-T-O-N or V-I-R-G-I-N-I-A.

As it came more clearly into focus in my teen years, I found the WASP ethos of Roland Park simultaneously fascinating and bewildering. I could never quite put my finger on it. Yet however indecipherable was its source code, in application it became something instantly familiar to me. As an adult, I would have the distinct sense whenever I watched the elder President Bush on television that I was seeing someone I had met before. When my brother-in-law Terry described him as "the ultimate Yalie," I knew exactly what he meant. Nowadays, a Yale man is more likely to be a Korean woman with perfect SAT scores, but not then. Terry didn't have to explain it. You knew. We all knew. These were the people "to the manner born," and we were keen if involuntary observers of the manner.

Boys' Latin was considered, by academic standards, on the third rung among the local prep schools, below Gilman and St. Paul's. By social standards, though, it wasn't even on the same ladder as the public school I attended as a boy.

I can still hear my friend Tyrone's voice as he stepped onto the school bus in the morning, singing "Hot Fun in the Summertime" just like Sly and the Family Stone. He was the fastest sprinter in my elementary school, and I was the fastest over distance. I remember how the sweat glistened on his skin during the races we ran together in the heat of Indian-summer afternoons. I think I knew, even then, that there wasn't anyone named Tyrone at Boys' Latin.

Two basketball hoops had been erected at opposite ends of the Boys' Latin parking lot, and I wore a groove in the concrete running between them. Every Christmas brought a new ball, and most mornings throughout the year I rose early to shoot for an hour or two before catching the school bus. I would shoot for another hour during recess, two more hours after getting home, and all day on Saturday.

Eventually, I could hit from anywhere on the court. No evening could end until I had hit ten shots in a row. As night fell, a lone spotlight from a nearby building threw off a dim glow behind the backboard. Eventually the hoop became a shadow and the swish of the ball dropping through the net my only clue to its location. Though I couldn't drive for a layup or jump worth a nickel (you don't acquire those skills playing by yourself), I was a 100-percent three-point shooter before there was such a thing as the three-point shot.

Although I was a fixture at Boys' Latin, even wending my larcenous way through the sumptuous buffet line at homecoming, I rarely talked to the kids who went to school there. My intimidation was largely a self-inflicted wound. I knew you had to take tests to get into the school, and I was sure that those who had been admitted were much smarter than I.

The Secret

They wore a uniform that set them apart, although their clothes were usually disheveled from after-school horseplay as they stood around waiting for the aforementioned Volvos to arrive. Most of those who hadn't gone home by the afternoon were on the field playing lacrosse—a game I did not know. Every once in a while, though, some kid who had missed his ride would wander down to the parking lot and make the mistake of challenging me to a game of one-on-one in basketball. A boy who fancied himself a player took it particularly hard when he lost. I remember what his classmate said to him as he urged him just to walk away: "Don't worry about it. That's all he does."

It wasn't all I did, by a long shot, and I wanted to say so. I wanted to say that I played jazz piano when I was supposed to be practicing Bach, that I loved to write and was a pretty fair shot with a bow and arrow, and that I knew exactly what the surface temperature of the water in Lake Roland had to be before the largemouth bass would begin to move into the shallows. But I also knew that these skills would be laughably beside the point. I wasn't part of that tribe. A child of an alcoholic is, in his own mind, the last surviving member of a lost civilization. He sees no point in trying to fit in with society at large, because he is certain he never will.

My mother combatively resisted such self-depravation. Her own father was a drinker, but she had an almost pugilistic confidence in her own potential and firmly believed in the American gospel of personal transformation. For her, the finer sensibilities of the upper classes were to be emulated, while their pretensions were to be avoided. Eleanor Roosevelt best embodied that balance for my mother and many others of her generation. A New Dealer to her grave, Mom felt a visceral aversion to the country club set even as she longed to experience the finer things that their intelligence and education had brought them.

And so she launched me like a deep-sea probe into their midst.

I was christened at three months of age in Baltimore's venerated old stone Cathedral of the Incarnation, known for the extravagance of smells and bells that are the mark of "high church" Episcopalians. At the first opportunity I was enrolled in the cathedral boy choir, where I and a restless horde of others were paid one dollar per month for the fleeting beauty of our soprano voices. Owing to my short stature and the length of a choir robe intended for a taller boy, there was a spectacular trip-and-fall incident involving a candelabra and a great deal of noise during the solemn procession of the choir at midnight Mass one year. Only my pride and the pageantry of the moment were damaged, but my memories of cathedral life mysteriously end there.

At age ten I went off for the first of two summers at a day camp at the McDonogh School, where 1930s Wimbledon champ Don Budge offered tennis clinics for delighted children, and cool college kids taught us the rudiments of English riding and jumping. How my mother found the money for this extravagance I have no idea. Alongside my peers, who were dressed in proper English riding hats, I clearly stood out—if not for my riding, then unmistakably for the shiny white miner's helmet I wore. It came free of charge from Mine Safety Appliances, where my mother worked as a secretary. No one except perhaps my horse was more astonished than I one summer when we were called into the ring to accept the first-place ribbon. It was my earliest experience of victory over my own diminished expectations.

Elkridge Estates, as our apartments were ostentatiously named, seemed to be mostly a place for well-to-do empty-nesters and gay divorcees. My mother's ambitions notwithstanding, it was clear we didn't fit in there, either. The younger residents drove natty sports cars and played squash at local clubs—except for one guy.

The Secret

Hank Bauer, manager of the 1966 World Series Champion Baltimore Orioles, lived in the second apartment down from ours. There was no missing him when he arrived in his conspicuously long white Cadillac. Though I later learned he had been a star in his own right for the Yankees as a younger man, he seemed more like us than the rest of our neighbors. I was a Junior Oriole at the time. Membership came with a wad of fifty-cent bleacher tickets, and I could name every starter on the 1966 team.

Rumors circulated about the famous man on our street who seemed rarely to be at home. When I came with a brand-new ball looking for an autograph one day, he appeared at the door of his apartment wearing a white undershirt. He had what I don't pretend actually to recall but would confidently guess was a can of National Bohemian beer in his hand. Had it been Brooks Robinson's autograph I might have hesitated, but Mr. Bauer was just my neighbor, and before long I had whacked that ball as hard as any other, never to be seen again.

Hank Bauer, alas, didn't notice any remarkable talent in the Junior Oriole living two doors up from him, and it was also becoming clear that at 5 feet 10 inches tall and 140 pounds, I was unlikely to star on any school's basketball team. About the same time those doors of my childhood were closing, however, another opened to me.

A man in his early forties named Crawford moved into the end unit of our building. Spotting me around the neighborhood, he invited me to test out a lacrosse stick made of urethane plastic in a new design that he and some fellow investors had just patented. It was going to be manufactured by a newly formed company named STX. I didn't know it then, but in the rarefied world of big-time lacrosse, that moment in history was something akin to the advent of Microsoft.

Mr. Crawford became a friend. My mother confided in him the story of our family, and he shared with us the story of his own father and mother. He was unmistakably a member of the elite tribe, but he had somehow escaped and learned to speak our language.

Before long, I was outfitted—free of charge—in all the lacrosse gear STX was selling at a premium to kids at Boys' Latin and other prep schools around the Northeast. I began practicing in earnest with the newfangled stick that would revolutionize the old-school game.

William Chauncey Crawford knew a thing or two about the old school. He was an All-American in lacrosse at the University of Virginia in the 1950s when sticks were still handmade of wood and strung with rawhide by Indians. He also did a stint on the admissions committee at Princeton. In that day, people would sometimes lament the number of applicants from elite private schools whose only distinguishing characteristic was the number of summers they had spent at Nantucket. Bill would beg to differ, and—to be fair—there were kids from public schools and modest backgrounds who made it into the Ivy League on their own merit. But I listened with interest and made the wrong mental index card: Nantucket. Vacation. Elite.

Mr. Crawford encouraged my mother to enroll me at Gilman and advance my prospects for acceptance at a better college, but I was hardly complicit in that plan. Traditional schoolwork held little interest for me, and my grades showed it.

Besides, by the time I was of high school age I had spent years balancing a chip on my shoulder and was rather good at keeping it there. Private schools and the social expectations that came with them seemed daunting. It never occurred to me, as it never does to adolescents of any generation, that every other child harbored some version of the same anxiety. I preferred to go my own way. Like most children of alcoholics, I had become skilled in the subterfuge necessary to protect "the secret."

The secret was that I had no father who was present in my life in any meaningful way. The secret was that my father had no job, no money, and was known to me mostly in the halfway houses where my mother and I would go to pick him up, straighten him out, and set him back on his feet with a few dollars in his pocket. The secret was that we lived in a one-bedroom apartment and not in a house that we had any prospect of owning. Keeping the secret as I was growing up meant that we had no significant friendships with families other than our own and that kids from school were never invited to my home for dinner. We were social ingénues, and I suppose it showed. Of course it showed.

Chapter 26

THE STORY

Every fall brought the ritual trip to the Jos. A. Bank men's clothing store in Towson. My mother and I would go in search of a new navy blazer, a button-down shirt, khaki pants, and a tie. Bank's was Baltimore's answer to Brooks Brothers. It was the place where mostly private-school kids, growing weedlike year to year, went to be outfitted in the college preparatory style at reasonable cost. I shall never forget the day—I must have been about fifteen—when the salesman making small talk while measuring my pant legs asked, "So, what does your dad do?"

I froze. It was a natural question—particularly in this part of town, where the answer to that question still mattered to many. This was also not the first time I had felt awkward in having to deal with the subject. But here, of all places, I wanted the answer to be different.

This was a time when the sporting, clubby lifestyle that is the beating heart of companies like Jos. A. Bank and L.L.Bean and Brooks Brothers had not yet been co-opted by discount department stores and merchandized to the masses by Ralph

Lauren and Abercrombie & Fitch. If you didn't know about these places or know someone who knew, you shopped at Stewart's or Hutzler's, perfectly content and none the wiser that your fashion choices were lighting up your family tree like a sign on the New Jersey Turnpike that said ALL FULLER BRUSH SALESMEN EXIT HERE.

Wearing a navy blazer from Bank's and a regimental tie, on the other hand, left open the possibility that you were having lunch with Her Majesty the Queen that day. The outfit said something unspoken but important about the person who wore it. It meant you knew. People who knew would see that you knew. It wasn't clothing. It was a totem. That was why we were there. We wanted to be in the tribe, and the salesman's question about my father was a demand that I demonstrate the secret tribal handshake.

How could I not have seen this coming? How could I have been caught so unprepared at my own game of subterfuge?

So I lied—sort of.

I told the man that my dad was a technical writer for Martin Marietta, the aircraft manufacturer that had a research facility in Baltimore. Dad had briefly held that job, I had been told, back in the fifties. He had long since moved on, been laid off, or been fired for not showing up—I never really knew. It was the last full-time job and the only steady white-collar job I was aware he ever had. Like all such stories in all alcoholic families, my dad's career as a technical writer was burnished and preserved to give me something "normal" to hang on to. It was an expired ID badge that I could use to get in the front door, if the doorman didn't look too closely. I hoped I would not be pressed for further details about my father's work, because I had none.

The pause in the salesman's reaction told me that my answer had not been fully satisfying, but it was enough of a diversion to move the conversation along. In the end, he did sell us the jacket and the pants.

For a long while, I hated myself for the answer I gave that day in Bank's and for others just like it. I hated the way the question made me feel, and I felt diminished by my grasping duplicity. I wished I'd had the courage to tell the truth, but I also understood why I did not.

At one time I had resolved to say that I came from an Irish Catholic alcoholic family, which I thought might somehow blunt the stigma of alcoholism with an air of heroic tragedy, as if being alcoholic and Irish Catholic were something akin to being a Kennedy. The Hurleys were Irish and Catholic, it is true, which is nothing like being a Swedish Methodist or a Dutch Presbyterian. It is rather more like being a Hungarian Jew, for whom religion is as much a matter of lineage as doctrine. It mattered not that my father had long ago fled the restrictions of Catholicism for the easier virtues of the Episcopal Church. He and his two brothers all died certifiably of the drink as had scores of Irish before them, no matter what their religion.

But I was also the product of French Protestants on my mother's side, who, I learned, could account for an equal number of drunkards of no lesser initiative. It seemed I was the genetic equivalent of a well-mixed drink—a rum punch of hidden, tragic possibilities.

The secret of my family and its power over me did eventually, and however slowly, begin to fade. A day finally came when I could look a stranger in the eye and say, "My dad was a drunk," without thinking that I was revealing something embarrassing about myself instead of something honest about him. I was in my forties by the time I could just let that one rip. If someone was daring or presumptuous enough to ask such a question, I decided, they had coming whatever discomfort the answer might bring. Not everyone's dad is well, after all, and if you take it upon yourself to go rummaging through people's closets, you mustn't be frightened when you encounter the odd skeleton.

Once I moved to the South, I discovered that skeletons in the family closet are regarded with an almost mischievous delight. Any true southerner would feel rightly deprived were there no old bones to be found lodged somewhere in his past. Southern Episcopalians especially, I have learned, are fairly rife with scandals going back generations. There is a kind of friendly competition among them as to whose spinster great-aunt was the bigger philanderer. I gave the my-dad-was-a-drunk answer once at a dinner party among such folk but failed to achieve my intended, retaliatory effect. I was gently corrected and politely informed that, in the South, one might often hear someone say his daddy was a drunk, followed invariably by the words "bless his heart."

Though the tentacles of one's upbringing may never fully release their grip, in my case they began at least to ease as I entered college. I gained a little of the confidence and much of the cockiness that most eighteen-year-old boys possess in overabundance. I discovered that I could cram and still pass the test. A pretty girl or two looked my way. Fraternity life gave me membership in a new kind of tribe that had nothing to do with my roots. My earlier encounter with Bill Crawford had also afforded me an opportunity I otherwise never would have had to look behind the veil into the inner sanctum of the Baltimore old-school elite, whose most sacred ritual is the game of lacrosse.

I never played with the natural fluidity of those who had come up in the Kelly Post leagues—carrying a stick almost since their first steps—but coming from strong peasant stock, I had the advantage that I could run till the barn fell down. By the time I was a freshman I had learned to handle a stick well enough to make the third string of my college team. Although I mostly warmed the bench, I had a share in the franchise. I basked in the pride of every win, and we won all the time. It's no secret why: our starting goalie was a brick wall.

He came from Boys' Latin.

Chapter 27

GATHERING STONES

My wedding and college graduation occurred within a span of two weeks in 1981. I was twenty-three. Besides my father, whose degree from Columbia in 1935 was the apex of an otherwise tragic life and the last gasp of his father's wealth during the Great Depression, at the time I was the only one on either side of my family for as many generations as anyone remembered who had graduated from college.

The significance of that day did not hit me until I saw my mother's excitement at commencement. It was as if the stone had been rolled away. A score had been settled. My cap and gown were a badge of normalcy not just for me but for her. I looked just like every other mother's son that day, and that was something new.

My bride-to-be came from the other side of the tracks on which I had so long fixed my gaze. A sorority president and the daughter of a rising corporate executive, she was only the latest of many college graduates, professionals, and business owners on both sides of her family. Anticipating that union with a looming sense of responsibility, I had spent the previous year cleaning up my act and retaking courses that I had bombed. I managed to revive my flagging GPA to an even 3.0 and gain admission to the midwestern law school that we would both attend.

Suddenly, with the wave of a priest's hand in a wedding ceremony, I was given a seat at the table in mainstream society. What had seemed far beyond my reach in the parochial wards of my childhood was now firmly in my grasp. I belonged to someone and something larger than myself. The old schoolboy prejudices and divisions were long forgotten and seemed rather silly in hindsight. I was instantly a grown-up. The narrow prism through which I had viewed the world as a child had shattered. From a new, wider perspective, it seemed that the entire world wished me well, and that wish was coming true.

Three years later, with a law school diploma in hand and a passing score on the Texas bar exam, I had finally put the lie to the doubts of my childhood. I came to understand the power of the law as the great leveler of men. The only people whose opinions about my abilities ultimately mattered sat on juries, not in exclusive clubs or on admissions committees. No matter what his father did, and regardless of whether he went to Dartmouth or State U., drove a Volvo or a Chevrolet, or lived in a mansion or a shack, every lawyer whom I encountered on the other side of a courtroom would stand or fall on his own merit, under the equal application of the law. It was the ultimate game of one-on-one, and I was winning.

The arrival of children brought further, unexpected transformations. With towheaded, blue-eyed babes in my arms, the whole world smiled at me, thought well of me, cleared a path for me, and extended me every kindness. I received not only these gifts but also the chance to travel back in time. My children's childhood was a do-over of my own. I got to be the father to them that I had never known.

All of this changed with startling abruptness one day, twenty-five years later.

Chapter 28

CASTING AWAY

Because so much of the person I had become for three decades was the propagation of changes begun with my marriage, leaving my marriage was like being ripped out by the roots. Though the bloom had fallen from that rose, the garden path was well traveled, and old habits were deeply planted. The trauma inflicted by the winnowing blade in my life was everywhere apparent.

I quickly realized that while I was suddenly a free man, I was also a branded man. What had happened to my marriage was the nightmare of wives everywhere. I became a hobgoblin of my married friends' darkest imagination. I was a traitor, a deserter, a quitter. People may be forgiven their mistakes and remarry when they are young, but a special contempt is reserved for men who leave a lifelong marriage when they are older.

The news of my divorce engendered sympathy initially, but when I began immediately to date other women, the sympathy of some turned to suspicion. Some no longer thought well of me, cleared a path for me, or extended me every kindness. Even some members of my own family turned their backs. My divorce was regarded as a kind of dread communicable disease. With children nearly grown and already hurtling down their separate paths, I was alone again. The old doubts returned. In the fading light of middle age, I was aiming for a rim I could no longer see clearly and missing it widely.

I also had a new secret. In an instant, I was once again that fifteen-year-old boy standing in the clothing store. The awkward question now was not about my father but about my wife. "So," any woman would naturally ask of a man divorced after twenty-five years of marriage, "what happened?"

Slicker at forty-eight than I was at fifteen, I could summon a catalog of convincing answers to that question—all of them poetic, all of them tragically endearing, all of them exculpatory, and all of them false to a greater or lesser degree. People who go through divorce and reenter the dating world often have elaborate cover stories about the failure of their marriages that they tell prospective partners. I heard some doozies. Mostly, they are just pep talks people give themselves to avoid confronting an uncomfortable reality. They are almost always variations on a familiar theme: it wasn't me; it was him (or her).

Just as it had taken me some time before I could tell the truth about my father, it was no easy task at first to tell the truth about my marriage. I remember when that moment finally came.

It had been more than a year since I had moved out. I was attending the first session of a support group with other newly divorced and separated people, mostly women, in a Baptist church classroom in Raleigh. One by one, we were asked to tell our stories. The only other man in our group had a story of heroic self-sacrifice that I couldn't touch. Then, after listening to a toe-curling litany of what "the bastard" had done to several of the women, I knew I had to come clean. Nothing less than the unvarnished truth would do.

And so the boy who had learned to let go of his shame and say

"My dad was a drunk" met the man who had to face up to his shame and say "I had an affair."

It was an ugly weed, and I knew it. Still, the women in the group seemed less offended by what I had done than they were intrigued by my honesty. A few commented that if their ex-husbands had only been capable of the same candor, they would still be together. This was encouraging, but as questions ensued and I struggled to mulch around that weed with context and explanation, it was clear to everyone, including me, that it would never become a rose. A weed it remained. There was no denying it, and for the first time, I no longer tried.

I began, in that moment of long-overdue candor, the steep road back. I began at last to heal, to let go, to forgive myself, and finally to understand some things about marriage.

Chapter 29

THE PASSAGE

It is well said that we ought not to judge a book by its cover. Once as a child rummaging through my mother's library, I discovered a volume with an ill-fitting jacket. The jacket described a text of some kind that I must have found interesting, because I opened it. Inside I was surprised to find a different book entirely, entitled *Advice from a Failure*, by Jo Coudert.

I didn't read it—as a child I certainly had no interest in anyone's advice—but as an adult I would learn that this was a popular self-help book, first published in 1965 and written by a woman who grew up in an alcoholic family. The fact that my mother felt compelled to hide the title with the jacket of another book speaks volumes about the deep emotional wounds suffered by many who come from such circumstances.

The memory of that book returned to me as I began to write this memoir. The title seems apropos, because what I have learned about marriage and what allowed me to face unafraid the prospect of marrying again did not come from someone else's good example or kind instruction. I learned those things the hard way—through my own failure.

The Passage

I had known as a child what it meant to be alone, to be uncertain, and to be vulnerable. I had grown up with those doubts, battled them, and won a decisive victory against them as a young man, only to see them return in my middle age to challenge me again. The trials and errors that had taken me to a moment of truth on the open sea east of Charleston on the morning of December 21, 2009, were painful, but they had restored my confidence in my own ability to choose a new heading.

Looking back, I see now that there probably was no easy passage for me around that Cape of Storms, just as there is likely no book with the title *Advice from an Unqualified Success*. I had to beat against the wind before I could learn to go around it. What I discovered along the way is a metaphor of sorts. A happy marriage and a good life, as it turns out, are one and the same. As you might have guessed in reading any letter of mine, I concluded that the pursuit of each is a thing very much like sailing.

To someone with neither the knowledge nor the patience to learn how helm, sails, wind, and waves work together in a symphony of forward movement, or who lacks the temperament to adapt to the constant, subtle changes in each, a sailboat is an impenetrable mystery and an object of frustration. Let your attention be long distracted from the helm of a boat or your marriage and you will surely run aground in either. But to one who understands the improvements in distance, direction, and speed that can be achieved through frequent small adjustments over time, such a vessel can take him in safety and comfort anywhere in the world, for as long as he lives.

No matter how fierce your ambition to do so, you cannot sail a boat directly into the wind any more than one spouse can vanquish the other in a contest of wills. The boat simply will not go. The sails will luff in disorderly and loud objection to that plan, and despite the illusion of progress amidst all the commotion, the vessel will make no way. But compromise and steer slightly off the wind, a few degrees to one side or the other of your intended mark, and the boat will come alive with purpose and movement. So it is in love.

There are, of course, limits to the metaphor. While every boat may be in need of only a willing captain and a fresh breeze, men and women are not made of timber and rigging. The same man or woman who thrives in one relationship may founder in another. Women in abusive marriages will find little encouragement in romantic allegories. There comes a time, whether on land or at sea, when the only sane course is to run from the storm and take shelter in the nearest port. Mutiny may be for some the most honorable course of action, and only a fool goes down with the ship.

There are men who taste the bitterness of their regret every day and who would tell you that their wives are intolerable shrews—cold, unloving, or indifferent to their dreams. For some poor devils perhaps this is so, but I would guess their bona fide numbers to be fewer than many believe. Some have never learned and others have forgotten that marriage is not a linear equation but a circular one, which is to say that "what goes around comes around." Marriage is influenced and will be changed by what we do just as the motion of a boat at sea is affected by the actions of her helmsman, who is himself affected by the motion of the boat, and so on. If he lets his ship veer off course, the captain will do himself little good to be shouting at the "damned boat." Husband and wife, hull and helmsman, are inextricably intertwined and rise or fall together.

Chapter 30

On Right Marriage

Never marry but for love; but see that thou lov'st what is lovely.

—*William Penn*

I have long admired the craft of the classical essayist, from Franklin and Thoreau to modern-day polemicists of all stripes, and I have sought in my own writing to emulate the best of them. One of the greats who must not be overlooked, in my opinion, is Colonial governor William Penn. In a collection of essays entitled *Some Fruits of Solitude*, published in 1682, he undertook to instruct a young nation clinging to the rough edges of a forbidding wilderness on, of all things, the finer points of "right marriage." That he spent far less time writing about the rudiments of farming or frontier living tells us something of the power to be found in the union of man and wife. That the great ships that bore Penn to our shores and the men who sailed them have all gone to dust, yet we today can still benefit from Penn's advice, tells us something of the power of the written word.

One need read no further than the title of Penn's essay to grasp the idea that there is such a thing as "wrong marriage." I once thought that when I had reached a certain age and experience, I, too, would weigh in authoritatively on this subject. I now imagine the angels and the saints, witnessing from above these high-minded intentions of an ignorant young man, and wonder how all of heaven contained the sound of their laughter.

Needless to say, I never qualified for my diploma in the instruction of others on the subject of marriage, right or wrong. But sailing south on a calm sea off the coast of South Carolina in the week before Christmas 2009, I confronted the necessity to apply what I knew.

I had met the woman whom I believed I would sorely regret not marrying, if I was given the chance and failed to seize it. As much as anyone, I could have found ample reason to be skeptical of my own judgment, yet I was certain of my heading. How is that so? I don't presume to answer that question for you, my friend, but I will tell you how I answered it for myself.

Since Governor Penn's day, it seems that our pursuit of the happily-ever-after has wandered off into adolescent navel-gazing. Nowhere is this more apparent than in computer matchmaking services, which perform a necessary and age-old function under a newly flawed premise. One such service proposes, for a breath-taking fee, to screen and combine its subscribers with would-be partners according to "29 Dimensions® of Compatibility." So revolutionary is this concept that the United States Patent and Trademark Office has seen fit to register the phrase by which it is now widely marketed to an eager and growing public.

In my view, the idea that compatibility governs our happiness and should be primary in our efforts to discern and choose a proper mate is self-seeking nonsense. A husband is not a pizza with twenty-nine available toppings. We do not order up a wife in the same way that we call for the daily deep-dish special, with pepperoni but not mushrooms, olives but not anchovies, and wait impatiently for her to be rushed to the altar, still hot and in thirty minutes or less.

The simple truth is that while we may find the perfect match when it comes to choosing a car, a house, or a suit of clothes, there is no such thing as a perfect match when it comes to choosing a mate. Only a narcissist seeks a mate who is a mirror image of himself. He may gaze at her awhile, love-struck, but when he realizes that her image is not his own, he will leave in frustration, only to continue his search for his "true love" in other mirrors. We see this continually in Hollywood, which is our national shrine to narcissism.

So long had I been pining for the perfectly compatible über-bride that it was something of an epiphany for me, in my middle age, to realize that she never existed. Human beings are unique, complex, and constantly changing, and no one is capable of meeting all the needs of another. The sooner we admit that fact, the happier we will be with ourselves and our spouses. Any plan for our happiness that depends upon finding such a person, and any marriage whose survival depends on the ability of that person to save us from the loneliness and want of every unmet need, is doomed to failure. Eventually, one must accept the proverb that "enough is as good as a feast" or be forever hungry. Not only can't we find someone who is perfectly adapted to every facet of our personality, but that's really not the point.

Imagine, if you will, walking into a restaurant for the first time. The place seems to be a real find—quaint, attractive, and tucked away in a convenient corner of your own neighborhood. You admire the romantic lighting. The seats are comfortable, and the waitstaff is attentive. Inquiring of the owner, you learn that this restaurant has been doing a brisk business for years and is well loved by the community. You wonder how it is possible you did not know of it until now.

Looking at the menu, you see many of your favorite foods. But then, as your eyes move down the side of the page, you see several more items that, frankly, are not your cup of tea. Mine would be beets. For others it may be creamed spinach. Perhaps for you it is chopped liver. For the sake of this example, let's say that beets, spinach, and liver are all on the menu, but so are garlic mashed potatoes, which you love. You order and are delighted to be served a delicious and satisfying meal.

Would you leave this restaurant and never return because it serves some dishes that are not to your liking? I think not. Would you circle the parking lot for years, checking reviews and ratings and coming in occasionally to sample another appetizer, before risking that you might be disappointed in a full meal? Or, having become a regular, would you walk out in a huff should the cook burn your favorite lasagna? I rather doubt it. You will be well fed here and you know it. The risk that the service may not always be impeccable or the food always delicious, or that not everything on the menu will be compatible with your taste, doesn't change that fact.

The comparison of spouses to soufflés is an awkward one, admittedly, but I believe that the choice of a mate can benefit from this example. Demand that nothing offend your sensibilities in any way and you will eat for the rest of your life at the International House of Pancakes. As for me, I prefer more adventurous fare.

Here is what I know: the one whom you would love has led a full life before she met you—which likely is part of what attracts you to her. In that span of time she has developed characteristics, interests, foibles, needs, and preferences dissimilar to your own. The question is not whether she will meet your every need or whether you can foresee and analyze correctly, in advance, every potential dimension of incompatibility. The question is not whether you are certain to be the answer to all her prayers. The question is whether, in each other's arms, you can find nourishment along with some of the variety that is the spice of life. If so, *bon appétit*.

On Right Marriage

Alas, though, this analogy has a darker side. While there may be no such thing as a restaurant that serves too little food or none at all, or whose offerings have become not merely dissatisfying but toxic, there are such marriages. You may once have been a devoted patron of such an establishment, and out of a sense of loyalty or charity or shame you may, for a time, pretend that you continue to be well fed there. Sooner or later, however, you must look elsewhere for nourishment or starve.

To these lofty remarks I add this final, grounding reality: If you believe, as I do, that marriage is a holy temple instituted by God, you must also accept, as many do not, that a time comes in some marriages when the money changers must be driven out. To imitate the sacrament of marriage by going through the motions of a relationship is to make a mockery of that sacrament. Divorce is a failure not to be wished upon anyone, but there is honesty in failure.

Chapter 31

A Mystery Unfolds

> The most beautiful thing we can experience in life
> is the mysterious. It is the source of all true art and
> science. He to whom this emotion is a stranger,
> who can no longer pause to wonder and stand rapt
> in awe, is as good as dead: for his eyes are closed.
> —*Albert Einstein*

One should be careful when listening to Van Morrison songs. Like the carriage that turns into a pumpkin at the stroke of midnight, in the blink of an eye "Crazy Love" can turn into just plain crazy.

It would have been easy to dismiss what I was feeling for Susan after just one weekend as I sailed south from Charleston—if not as crazy, then as simply foolish. But to dismiss such feelings is to be dead to the possibility of mystery. I don't presume necessarily to understand my life as it occurs, but I know that I must experience it in real time, not in hindsight. Grace often comes to us as an angel in strange disguise, and we must have the courage to welcome the stranger.

At six in the evening on my first day at sea, after leaving Charleston, I sat down to write Susan a letter. All was quiet, the new winter sun had already set, and in the soft glow of the cabin where only two days before we had danced and talked long into the night, the sense that my life had just changed greatly for the better covered me like a warm blanket.

"Like a child at Christmas," I wrote to her, "I may not know all that the future holds, but I have a childlike sense of wonder, awe and excitement, and an innocent faith that what waits for us is something beautiful to behold." I think this may have been what Mr. Einstein was trying to tell us, and it is definitely what I believe.

As I wrote those words I was already far out of sight of land. An unseen school of fish—perhaps tuna or mahimahi—went rushing under my keel, setting off the depth alarm and reminding me that there were forces busily at work beneath the placid surface of the ocean. The same was true of my thoughts, which raced expectantly beneath my calm exterior. Big changes were on the way, and I was about to make them.

In the hours I had spent trying to evade Charleston two weeks earlier, I had gained a greater understanding of the operation of the Monitor self-steering wind vane. Though the electronic autopilot had since been repaired, I now used the mechanical wind vane for self-steering exclusively. With nothing but wide miles of ocean between me and the Berry Islands, I had unfettered, quiet hours to fill with thoughts and written words.

I made good time, covering 115 miles in the first day. In that distance I saw not one other vessel on the open sea. I also remained out of communication with land. Cell phones and VHF radios cannot receive a clear signal farther than twenty-five miles from shore. There were no VHF weather reports. There was only the sound of my ship moving through the water, her rhythmic creaking and groaning becoming as regular and familiar to me as a heartbeat.

"Were it not for your picture," I wrote to Susan, "I might be tempted to believe it was all a dream. Perhaps the sea was playing tricks on me, and I have really been on the same long trip the whole time."

The sea's tricks would come soon enough. But for now, there was time to write, and I had a lot to say. It was not loneliness that compelled me to dwell on these things, but a quiet resolve.

"Perhaps it is just as well that we have this time," my letter continued, "to contemplate what it is we are about to begin. In my contemplation... I am struck by how different you are... There is nothing 'hard' about you... You have a gentleness, a softness that is so disarming and endearing. There is no sarcasm or bitterness or edge of anger, in your voice. You seem to go lightly through life, and I am eager to follow."

The sea was like glass on the second night, which turned out to be, as it usually is, a sign that the weather would soon change. By the third day I was off the coast of Florida, and by nightfall I was passing south of Daytona Beach about sixty nautical miles northeast of Cape Canaveral. Here, on December 23, I was finally able to pick up a weather forecast.

"The wind is due to clock to the southwest on Christmas," I wrote to Susan, "right on time for the crossing." I had planned to jut across the Gulf Stream at its narrowest point, when I was abeam of West Palm Beach, and glide into the pale blue water of the Bahama Banks on my way to Nassau. "Everything has gone perfectly on the trip thus far, including the very necessary failure of my autopilot, followed promptly by my engine transmission..."

A trio of dolphins swam alongside the *Gypsy Moon* for a long while that afternoon. I also briefly glimpsed what I couldn't be sure but suspected, due to its size, was a breaching whale. Suddenly the ocean was coming alive, and so was the wind. I felt more keenly the change that was in the air. "Strangely," I wrote that night, "I don't wish you were here. The sea has its dangers, and I want to keep you safe by my side..."

With the boat making good time and now in range of cell towers, I sent an all-is-well text message to Susan and my family and friends, predicting that I would cross the Gulf Stream into Bahamian waters the next day. That turned out to be wishful thinking.

By the morning of the fourth day, Christmas Eve, the weather had shifted to the southwest with a vengeance. There would be no letter to Susan or Santa that day, because the motion of the boat in the rising wind and seas was so labored that it was impossible to hold a pen steadily enough to write.

Once again, I found myself crawling forward on deck, preparing to raise the storm trysail that I had thought I'd never use. I well remember the scene. I paused for a moment to marvel at the size of the waves on the same ocean that had been a mirror two days before, and I imagined what I would look like to someone watching me on a television set from the safety of his living room—like a crazy man, I decided.

The trysail had its intended effect, but even with the calming of the motion of the boat, every line and halyard seemed to be as tight as piano wire under the strain. Despite the strength of the wind that should have been driving her forward, with her sails shortened the *Gypsy Moon* was now in a contest of wills with the large rollers coming at her from the south. Our speed slowed to a crawl, and my attention again turned to the weather forecast.

According to the NOAA, I now had one day to make it to my intended turning point at West Palm Beach before the wind shifted to the north and closed the door to any attempt to cross the Gulf Stream. I suddenly had the sensation of déjà vu. This far south, the Gulf Stream runs only a few miles offshore. To avoid it, I was forced to tack back and forth with regularity in the narrow alley that runs between the west wall of the stream on one side and the beaches on the other. While the wind vane could steer the boat without my aid, tacking and resetting the vane after each turn was a hands-on job.

By nightfall on Christmas Eve, I was exhausted from working the helm, to say nothing of how Santa and his reindeer must have felt in that headwind. I was increasingly in need of sleep, but I had less than an hour of time on each tack before I would need to come back out on deck and tack again to avoid being carried off in the Gulf Stream to the east or crashing into the lobby of some beachfront hotel to the west.

Up at the bow, the *Gypsy Moon* continued her fistfight with the waves as one steep rolling punch after another slammed into the hull, slowing our speed made good (the distance over the bottom) to less than three knots. By midnight on Christmas morning, the wind speed was gusting to twenty-six knots and the boat had reached an effective stalemate in her contest with the sea: tall waves kept coming north, and we weren't moving any farther south.

A change in plans was needed. I fell off the wind and ran five miles out to sea in an effort to get some speed going under the hull before tacking back toward the coast on a wider broad reach. This approach meant I was sailing a less due-southerly angle in exchange for greater boat speed that I hoped would let me make more southward progress against the waves. With the boat on a comfortable heading, I set the egg timer alarm and nodded off in my bunk down below.

Every sailor at some point, if not often, realizes that he has benefitted from the vigilance of an unseen crew. In his book about becoming the first man to sail alone around the world in 1898, Joshua Slocum shared the credit with the long-dead pilot of Christopher Columbus's ship the *Pinta*, whose ghost Slocum matter-of-factly claimed he saw steer his sloop whenever he was most in need of aid.

A Mystery Unfolds

I saw no ghost of Christmas past or present that night off the coast of Florida, but I was mighty glad for whatever (or whoever) awakened me well ahead of my alarm. Coming out on deck early, I was startled to see that the depth sounder read only twenty feet instead of sixty. Judging from the glare of the lights onshore and the sound of breaking waves, the beach could not have been far from my bow. On a broad reach in the rising wind, the boat had made much better speed than I had expected. She was racing toward shore, and with a few more minutes of sleep, I would have parked her neatly in some child's sand castle.

With hands shaking and heart pounding, I quickly spun the wheel around to put the helm on an easterly heading. The rowdy wind sent the boom and mainsail crashing to leeward. I had nearly made a mistake that would have cost me the *Gypsy Moon* and put an end to my dreams for good. "What would Susan have thought of such a blunder?" I wondered.

I took a step back and tried to look objectively at my situation. I was not far enough south yet to attempt a Gulf Stream crossing. Once I entered it, the stream would carry me well north of my position, and at this latitude, wherever I came out on the other side I would miss the Bahama Banks entirely. I needed to make another 125 miles of southing before I could turn, but at the present speed that would take three days. In less than one day the wind was forecast to turn to the north and increase to thirty knots, where it was supposed to remain for a week. In those winds, the Gulf Stream would be an impassable war zone. The mantra I knew best was that no crossing could be attempted in a north wind.

Exhausted again, I hove to the boat on an offshore heading and waited till the dawn of Christmas Day. I was just below the hook of Cape Canaveral, and glancing at the chart book, I saw that there was a full-service marina nearby.

143

You know for sure that you're all grown up when you're motoring alone into a deserted marina on Christmas morning. I had made the choice to be there, it was true, and I would have been just as alone back in my apartment in Raleigh, but there is never a better opportunity to feel sorry for oneself than to be the only one in a shipyard on Christmas. Or so I thought.

I had forgotten that whenever I am around boats and seawater, there will always be someone, somewhere, who suffers my addiction. In this case, the fellow was easy to spot in an ancient wooden Colin Archer sloop that was a throwback to the days of Joshua Slocum I had only recently called to mind. He was sailing for Maine with a rather interesting and odd sort of crew (they are always interesting and odd), but I could not have wished for a nicer bunch to greet me on Christmas morning.

The only unlocked public bathrooms with hot showers at the marina were coin operated, and there was no coin changer within walking distance—not that it would have mattered, as I had nothing less than a ten-dollar bill to change. One of the crew on the Colin Archer took pity on me. Extending an arm tattooed over its entire length, he opened his hand to empty a stack of quarters into mine and then said: "As they say in the Middle East, go with God."

It was a merciful gift. God and I went straightaway, as directed, and got a wonderfully hot shower.

The next morning, the red and green Christmas lights came on early in the marina store, and I made arrangements for dockage for the *Gypsy Moon* until I could return. After spending five days at sea since leaving Charleston, it seemed impossible that I would be stopped again, short of my destination, but there I was.

The marina hands directed me from the fuel dock where I had tied off the day before to a slip on one of the interior piers. As I secured the *Gypsy Moon* in her temporary home, I noticed that the boat in the slip next to her seemed to be a somewhat more permanent fixture. Looking closely, I saw that this little boat, a day sailor no more than seventeen feet long, with only kneeling headroom, was the homestead of a middle-aged Latina who lived alone. Her grandchildren had come to visit her on the day after Christmas.

When those of us who have lived lives of relative abundance and ease see such scenes, we are often moved. On that morning after Christmas, I was moved not by a sense of anyone's hardship or despair but by the genuine contentedness of this woman to be living in that place, in what most of us would regard as difficult circumstances, without any evidence of difficulty.

I had a shipful of stores that I was not likely to need anytime soon. One by one, I lifted plastic bags filled with cans of food over the side of the woman's boat until it could hold no more. She spoke no English. In broken Spanish, I established that she liked *vino rojo* and gave her the few bottles I had left to wash down the ravioli. I explained the troubles of wind and weather that had brought me to that place. She was gracious in acknowledging her need, and I was honored to be able to give someone an unexpected gift in person that Christmas.

Chapter 32

An Immodest Proposal

"It feels strange to be writing this... to you on the tray table of an airplane," my next letter to Susan began, on December 26, 2009. "I never expected to be where I am today—flying home on the wind to see you, instead of sailing on the wind farther from you. But then, life is like that. Things happen—beautiful things—when we least expect them... I didn't expect the *Gypsy Moon* to be stopped in her tracks by a Christmas Eve storm, but neither did I expect to be stopped and stunned by a 'date' I had in Charleston one week ago."

By then, I think we both knew that what had occurred the week before was much more than a date. It was an opened door, and I was now hurrying back to the welcome that waited for me there. I had something to say to Susan. I wanted to tell her that my prayers had been answered, in hopes that her answer would be the same, but I needed to find the words. A letter would help me begin, and so I kept writing:

"I think many times we pray with little faith that God will actually grant us exactly what it is we seek, if anything at all. This sense of doubt can be so strong that when prayers are answered, and the very blessing that we hoped for arrives at our door, we assume it must have come to the wrong address."

I knew when I stepped off the airplane in Charleston and saw a woman waiting there, her smile beaming down the Jetway at me, that I had come to the right address and that the *Gypsy Moon* had known her proper heading through that Christmas gale far better than her captain.

Nassau would have to wait, again. It was well that I had turned back, as a strong north wind was now blowing and would continue to blow into mid-January. Had I somehow made it all the way to Nassau, I would have missed Susan's birthday—her fifty-first—the day after Christmas. As it was, the only gifts I had to give her that day were my hand and heart, but she took them without hesitation and refused ever to give them back. Her answer, thanks be to God, was yes, and with that acceptance she banished every doubt I'd ever had about the power of Providence to see us through.

LATITUDE 28.40.88 N

LONGITUDE 80.62.73 W

PORT CANAVERAL, FLORIDA

Chapter 33

A Boy's Will

Four months would pass after my return to Raleigh from Port Canaveral in late December 2009 before I would see the *Gypsy Moon* again. In that brief interval, events in my life streaked past like leaves in a gale.

I had arrived back in Raleigh engaged to be married to a woman whom I had not known when I left. Two months later, I found a little yellow house that would become our new home on a leafy street in the suburbs and raided the remnants of my retirement savings for a down payment. In the meantime, Susan sold most of what she owned, ended a twenty-year career with the City of Charleston, and prepared to move north.

Longfellow wrote that "a boy's will is the wind's will, and the thoughts of youth are long, long thoughts." I had begun my voyage south in the variable winds and slack tide that followed the slow ebb of a twenty-five-year marriage. My decision to embark had been the final expression of a boy's will that his life should find some deeper meaning. I faced a sea of doubts in my search for what was certain and solid and true. Now, with Susan by my side, Longfellow's lament was no longer my own. An older and wiser man had at last taken the boy by the hand, steadied him, and set him upon the way forward.

When I piloted the *Gypsy Moon* out of Charleston Harbor to sea and the outer limits of wireless transmission on December 21, 2009, Susan's last words, "I am totally committed to you," had been all the more powerful for their unguarded simplicity. That unconditional sentiment had not been expressed to me by another woman in my life. Now that I was back ashore and in the earnest beginnings of a new year, I intended to make good on her commitment and match it with my own.

Improbably, new cases and fresh funding for my law practice came rolling in the door in spring 2010, and not a moment too soon. My cupboards had been nearly bare, but by the same mysteries I have witnessed all my life, the Good Lord again placed bread on my table in spite of my considerable efforts to interfere. With my workload suddenly mounting, I took out an advertisement that attracted the welcome interest of two young attorneys who helped me transform a sleepy solo practice into a respectable law firm. I found the perfect building, where I could lease expanded office space not three miles from the house Susan and I had chosen, and she and I prepared to begin a new life together with a vigor I had all but forgotten.

A young writer for a weekly newspaper that circulates among the state's lawyers became intrigued by the story of Susan's fairy-tale romance and decided to tell the world, as it were, in a front-page feature about a sailing attorney waylaid by a storm who came home with a bride. Good wishes followed from friends new and old, and the sun suddenly seemed a little brighter and higher in the sky. I planted roses in the garden of the little yellow house where we would begin our life together in August. But long before the wedding pipes might sing, there was a decision to make and a voyage to complete.

Chapter 34

A Moment of Truth

Sailing is an odd thing, and sailors by and large are an odd lot. As a manner of transportation the sailing vessel is ponderously slow, but as a means of impoverishment it is deceptively fast. Sailcloth is woven in gold mines, halyards are knit together by feather-winged angels, and bottom paint is made from rare, fine wine.

In beginning a new life, I was loath to ask my bride to bear the burdens that had weighed so heavily on my first marriage, chief among which was an expensive passion that my partner did not share with equal enthusiasm. I resolved to give up the ship before repeating that mistake.

Susan, like many people I have met who hear that I have a boat and that I venture about to various places far from land, was intrigued by the idea of sailing. But the imagining and the doing of things can be very different, and never has that been truer than when it comes to sailing offshore.

Most guests temporarily aboard the *Gypsy Moon* have found little not to their liking. She is a snug home, encircled in warm teak, with tufted cushions, standing headroom, and a charmingly simple layout. From her serviceable galley I have brought forth many candlelit dinners, lovingly prepared and served. Such an evening—played out in the serene setting of a moonlit harbor, accompanied by Sinatra, Bennett, or, perchance, a Van Morrison tune for dancing—can be a strong magic. Susan was no less enchanted and herself so much more enchanting than all the others who had fallen under the *Gypsy*'s spell, but I had more in mind for her. And because I did, I had no intention of taking Susan to that place where the spell of romantic harbors would be rudely broken.

Susan would get no invitation from me to go voyaging around the world. It is one thing to endure a hardship of one's own choosing but quite another to choose a hardship for someone one loves.

Far out at sea, days removed from the memory of a hot shower, a level surface, and a toilet that does not stand tauntingly on edge, defying the laws of gravity necessary for its use, there is no romantic thrall that can endure. In my years of bachelorhood, on those few occasions when I heard a woman's voice, in whispers and kisses, speak the words "I will go round the world with you," I heard the unspoken voice of reason in ready rejoinder say: "Alas, my dear, you will not."

Now, before any paper and ink are wasted on cries of sexism, I hasten to add that I speak here in generalities, not particularities. There are, I wager, at least a hundred women at sea this very hour who could take tea and biscuits in the gale that would send me whimpering to the lifeboats, but I don't care to marry any of them, and no doubt the feeling is mutual.

Selling the boat, I resolved, would not be such a bad thing. Perhaps it was time. The world of wind and sea was not Susan's dream, and I wondered whether it should any longer be mine. The vacuum in which I had begun the voyage had, after all, been filled. I was no longer living an outward metaphor of a solitary inward journey. I had reached my Ithaca at last. Perhaps the day had come for me to lie upon my laurels, meager as they were, and enjoy a long-awaited rest.

I did exactly that for a time, but as you no doubt suspect, there is more to this story. Always in the corners of my mind the image remained of my little boat, tugging at her lines, waiting to be off. A still, small voice in my head pleaded to go with her, as impractical as that now seemed.

For a time, reason prevailed over all emotion and small voices, still or otherwise. I did actually and in good faith put the boat up for sale. Several would-be owners bent my ear with intricate questions about her design and capacities for this or that, but they were never in the game to go. I tried to explain that here was a ship that had the heart of a vagabond and the means to fulfill the seduction she promised to men who looked longingly her way. Some listened intently but without real understanding. I answered their questions instead about the number of people the boat could sleep (five altogether, but only two in comfort); whether she had a hot and cold shower (she has neither); and whether she was wired for Internet and cable TV (blessedly, she is not).

I breathed a sigh of relief when no suitable offers came my way. The *Gypsy Moon* was saved from a sad fate as a floating South Florida condominium. But that didn't solve my problem, as I understood it at the time.

I found myself considering a donation of the boat to a church camp on the North Carolina coast, where it undoubtedly would have found a happy home. A man planned to come to my office to discuss details of retrieving the boat from Florida and bringing it north, where boys and girls would use it to learn to sail on their summer vacations—a worthy cause indeed.

The night before my meeting with the kind gentleman from the camp, I could not settle my thoughts. I finally confessed to Susan that I was not sure I had the will to let the *Gypsy Moon* go. Something in me resisted the idea. It was a fear, as best I can describe it, that I was giving up on myself and losing something that I would never get back. We all face these kinds of decisions in our lives, and often the moment of truth is not something we can avoid or forestall. We grow up. We leave. We change. We move on because we must. The nature of life is that it progresses inexorably in only one direction.

But this was different. This was a choice, not the passing of an epoch. And it was a choice about which I was unsure until Susan spoke her mind.

"Keep it," she said. "You've always sailed," and she was right. She reasoned that I needed at least one thing in my life that was all my own and that I loved to do. Sailing seemed to be that thing for me.

As Susan spoke these words, I felt a glacier thaw and a great burden fall away. The message that it was okay to be the man I am was both revelation and validation. I needed no revision or refurbishment as a condition of Susan's acceptance. My voyage would be acknowledged, accommodated, and celebrated between us. Had I demanded as much by stubborn force of will, the treasure she now offered would have slipped through my hands. But instead, Susan had freely opened her heart and made a home there for the dreamer and his dream.

The next day, with some embarrassment but no shortage of determination, I told the man from the summer camp of my change of heart. He was surprisingly supportive, and I dare say he'd even seen it coming. He told me that he had faced similar decisions and reached similar conclusions in his own life, and that he understood. It was okay. I had his permission as well to be exactly the person I wanted to be.

Chapter 35

A Plan in Earnest

Susan's blessing to follow my dream was like a strong wind at my back. I now had Nassau in my sights with a zeal and single-mindedness unknown to previous legs of the voyage. I planned to set sail from Port Canaveral on the second day of April 2010.

Passing through the airport on my way to Florida, I spotted a woman who knew me, my ex-wife, and our children fairly well and who herself was recently divorced after a long marriage. Her children and mine attended the same Catholic school. But still in that strangely adolescent phase of awkwardness that the newly divorced must endure, we pretended not to recognize each other as we walked past. She would not fail to notice that I was traveling alone, headed out of town on a pleasure trip in shorts and flip-flops without the fiancée whose engagement had just been announced to dozens of our mutual friends.

Not long after my plane landed in Florida, a rare and welcome unsolicited text message arrived from my teenage daughter, inquiring as to my well-being and whereabouts. I wondered but never asked whether there was some connection between the message and the woman in the airport, but regardless, there was no need for alarm. I was not running away from home. On the contrary, I was running headlong toward something I could now see clearly, and I had never been more certain about anything in my life.

For at least ten minutes.

With a rented car, I traveled around Port Canaveral to gather the usual impedimenta of an ocean voyage aboard a small sailing vessel. This included great quantities of bottled water, canned food, and items from a running list of common stores from the local ship chandlery. I must tell you, however, that I can scarcely bear these preparatory errands. In fact, I dread them.

Shopping for an extended voyage brings on a tinge of melancholy in me, as though I were a condemned man gathering victuals for a last meal. Nothing is surer to cause me to question why on earth I am heading out, alone, to endure the deprivations of life at sea than to be in a marketplace among happy families who are safe, warm, and dry and have nothing to fear. Their contented smiles convey a clear message to my imagination: "We are sane, and clearly you have lost your mind."

I have a ready antidote, however, for this malaise. I imagine myself an old man, reclining in an armchair, no longer able to move with ease. I have the same inclination to go traveling over the horizon as I do now, but I cannot. A woman I do not know listens politely as I tell the story of the solo voyage I almost made to a distant South Sea island. It is a place, I explain, that I would have and could have reached—not easily, mind you, but with some effort—aboard a well-found sailing vessel I used to own. Awkwardly, I reach into the pocket of my robe, retrieve a weathered photograph of the *Gypsy Moon*, and strain to bring it to the woman's attention. She smiles distractedly, fluffs my pillows, and writes a note for the doctor about checking Mr. Hurley's medications for hallucinatory side effects.

In that imaginary moment I am warm, safe, and dry—just like the crowd—but unhappily so, and with nothing to fear but the memory of what might have been.

Chapter 36

TO SEA AT LAST

Do you know how a voyage begins? By untying a line.

So it is when we begin our life on Earth. At first the umbilicus and then the apron strings are parted, and we leave our mothers. These necessary acts foreshadow all that follows. Nothing that is tethered can grow and survive.

Untying the lines at Port Canaveral, I was soon underway among the behemoth cruise liners that gather in this port, awaiting passengers. The road between here and Orlando is a tourism pipeline that each year carries thousands of people to an experience of ocean voyaging vastly different from the one I was about to encounter. Passing beneath the enormous bows of these ships in the broad terminal canal, I had a sense of myself as David in the shadow of Goliath. But my feelings of vulnerability would soon be swallowed up by the immensity of the ocean itself, whose breadth and depth make every boat a bath toy by comparison. Indeed, ships the size of these would soon be no more than pinpoints of light in the darkness on the vast night sea that lay between me and the Bahamas.

Taking a sailing ship through a channel out to sea is, I imagine, something like taking a Thoroughbred to the starting gate. In the initial going, there is a slow and ordered calm. The steady march that leads to the winner's circle is, as it begins, indistinguishable from the one that leads to the glue factory. But the rider knows where he is headed, and with a studied tension he anticipates the swell of movement that is about to erupt beneath him. Then the bell sounds, the traces fall away, and the Thoroughbred emerges in all his power to claim what is rightly his: the race to be run.

So it is with a ship. She is often necessarily in a safe harbor or a protected channel, but that is neither her home nor her element. She was made for the open sea, and the man or woman who would follow her there must prepare for the same. When the bow edges past the shelter of the breakwater and first encounters the unbridled power of nature, the helmsman's heart may pause, but the well-found ship joins the fray without hesitation—dipping her shoulder to the waves and turning the ocean's energy into speed and distance run.

Chapter 37

THE CROSSING

I was struck again as I left Port Canaveral by the expansive flatness of the Florida landmass. From the sea in daylight it appears to be scarcely there and could be missed entirely but for the long formation of hotels whose ranks lead all the way to Miami, broken only by the occasional inlet. It was midafternoon, and I was running on a reach down the coast, about five miles off.

My plan on this day in April was as it had been on that cold Christmas Eve in December—to stay within a few miles of the coast until I was well south of West Palm Beach, then break away for the Bahamas, arriving south of West End on my way to Nassau by way of the Berry Islands. With the assurance of a gentle southwesterly breeze, I put the diesel engine to bed as soon as I was safely clear of the channel at Port Canaveral. All sails were brightly flying, and my little ship was pulling hard for glory.

Anyone planning to cross the Gulf Stream cannot help but be awed by the tidal wave of advice awaiting the eager student of navigation. Being so close to the US mainland and within reach of hordes of weekend boaters, the Gulf Stream and its proper approach between the Bahamas and Florida are the subject of intense and constant editorial comment on the Internet. In these forums, wave heights, wind speeds, and navigational algorithms are hotly debated by anonymous admirals from the safety of suburban bedrooms. The certain calamity that awaits the uninformed is darkly described amid a cross fire of rejoinder and rebuttal until even the most careful reader can discern no safe path across the abyss.

Having studied all the available wisdom, I had a simple plan: to avoid turning into the Gulf Stream until I was far enough south that, turning east, I would hit my mark farther north on the other side, dead-on. By this method, crossing the stream is like shooting a bird on the wing. Aim directly at the bird, and by the time the bullet arrives, the target will be too far ahead. If a boat turns east too soon, the Gulf Stream will set it far to the north of its desired latitude. For this reason, it is necessary to make extra southing first, in order to make sufficient easting later, i.e., to aim the boat well below its intended landfall in the islands as though the entire Bahamas were a fat goose flying south for the winter.

It was a wonderful plan, but like so many other well-formed plans, it turned out ultimately not to apply. In fact, I slept through most of it.

By the time I came abeam of West Palm Beach, barely on latitude with the northernmost corner of Grand Bahama Island, the southwesterly breeze had blown me well offshore. To compound matters, West Palm is almost exactly the point at which the coast curves inward and westward on a slope toward the Florida Keys. To stay obediently on a course close to shore, I would have had to tack west and wait before crossing, and this is exactly what the experts would have advised.

In the end, I said good riddance to "the plan," threw the helm to leeward, prepared to cross the blasted stream at a sharp angle (verboten, say the experts), and decided to let the devil take the hindmost.

Now, I should here acknowledge to any who might carelessly follow my example that there are several reasons why the prudent mariner should be cautious about crossing the Gulf Stream. A friend and I once had a raucous sleigh ride from West Palm to Little Bahama Bank, trying to beat a spring wind that was clocking north as fast as we were sailing east. There are wooly-bully waves in the stream, to be sure. But for the life of me, I cannot tell you where they were that night in April as I was bound from Port Canaveral, because I hit the rack.

If necessity is the mother of invention, the Monitor Windvane self-steering gear must have been designed by a desperate insomniac. I have never been so gently rocked to sleep as aboard my own boat with old Mo at the helm. On that night, after I bore off to the east and tucked myself into the pilot berth, so steady was the helm that I scarcely stirred at all save for an occasional brief sleep-muddled gaze above the companionway at the dark horizon. More surprising, though, was the apparent absence of any significant swell during the crossing. I was still waiting for those rowdy bouncers to roll me out of bed when I realized that I was indeed safely and serenely in the shelter of the Bahamas. The *Gypsy Moon* had made the passage without much ado.

Chapter 38

ATLANTIS RISING

Taking my position via satellite in the hours just before dawn, I was astonished to realize that the current of the Gulf Stream had barely set me to the north at all. Under the wind vane, I had sailed sixty miles or more on a relatively straight southeast line across the stream. The southwestern cape of Grand Bahama Island was now bearing two points off my port bow. I was on my intended heading for the Berries.

Although a comfortable harbor at West End on Grand Bahama Island was a short sail away, I dismissed the idea of making port anywhere but Nassau. It would be fitting that I should land there and nowhere else after leaving Florida. Besides, the *Gypsy Moon* was sailing like a champion, and the entire ocean was ours. The petty entanglements and precautions of making landfall would become necessities soon enough. For now, I just wanted to sail.

The moment when I first realized that I would indeed complete a solo voyage to Nassau recalled for me the day when I first realized that I would actually—not theoretically or on some hypothetical future date—graduate from college. Both goals had at one time grown to mythic proportions in my mind. Both had remained well beyond my grasp after first attempts, and early timetables for their achievement had been wildly optimistic. It never occurred to me that I might actually pass the portals of higher education until the day I stumbled through to the other side, and I am not sure I truly believed I would ever step off my own boat onto the streets of Nassau until I had done just that. But first, there was still the matter of a hundred and forty miles of ocean to cross.

My euphoria ran high when I saw the water of the Bahama Banks glowing neon blue in the low light of dawn. I was well on the way to my destination. The next morning would be Easter. I still carried within my hold a book about the history of Raleigh's Christ Church, taken aboard five months earlier to be a gift to the parishioners of Christ Church in Nassau, though the pastor probably had abandoned any serious expectation of actual delivery. I kindled a tiny flame of hope that I might arrive in time to deliver this gift at the Easter vigil. That, too, would prove overly optimistic.

Morning waned into afternoon and afternoon into another night at sea. The *Gypsy Moon* was sailing well. Now, however, I did not have the reassurance of ample sea room to let her run. I slept in fits and starts of only minutes at a time or not at all between trips to the cockpit to mark my position, tack, and adjust my heading. By now I had picked up the easterly trade winds, and they were blowing with characteristic gusto. The boat was sailing on her ear to windward. I was luffing every sheet to ease the weather helm and calm the motion of the boat, but I knew the rise in wind speed was merely a temporary effect of thermal inversion from nearby land. There was no weather on the horizon. Besides, I was too eager to reach Nassau and too excited about the swift pace of the boat slicing through the night sea to shorten sail.

So fast did the old *Gypsy* run, in fact, that I could not in my night blindness easily gauge how close she was coming to the shallows in

the lee of the Berry Islands, where no boat can be assured of sufficient depth outside well-marked channels. As a result, I was tacking
sooner rather than later to be safe in the straits south of Grand Bahama. Nothing, after all, is more frightening in a boat with four feet
of draft than three feet of water.

By dawn of the third day at sea, Easter Sunday, my vigil was
nearly complete. I could now well see the sandy shores of the low-
lying Berry Islands to starboard and a few boats coming in and out
of Great Harbour Cay. Ahead in the distance, a large freighter appeared to be making way toward Nassau, but when I poked my
head into the cockpit again after breakfast, I was less than a mile
from her stern and closing fast. She was at anchor, not underway,
and out of a hundred miles of ocean I had somehow managed to
choose a collision course. I quickly came about and left her to starboard, reminding myself never to assume that a ship on the horizon
is underway until that assumption is verified by time and distance.

The Berry Islands have a reputation as a rich man's paradise: I
knew I had to leave the *Gypsy Moon* somewhere, and I had flirted
with the idea of leaving her at an elegant new resort on Chub Cay,
shown in pictures to be painted in saltwater taffy hues, but the
prices there were too dear. Besides, I was looking forward to settling
into the vibe of Nassau—a city that still held for me all the campy
mystique of late-night James Bond movie marathons from my childhood. I could not have been more excited.

The coral-colored spires of the Atlantis resort appeared to rise
higher from the sea with each mile I made south toward New Providence Island. At first I could not be sure of what I was seeing—a
storage tank onshore or another ship, perhaps—but as the architec-
ture rose farther skyward it became unmistakable. There would be
no occasion for sleep this night. I was very close to Nassau by sun-
set, and I would make the harbor long before sunrise.

Nassau still appears in some areas today as it did to the eye of Winslow Homer, who found the city a rich subject for his work in the 1890s. Approaching from the north, I struggled to see the dim glow of the old lighthouse at the harbor. Homer had depicted this scene in 1899 as viewed from the shore, looking north, where abandoned cannons were scattered on the sand. When I was finally within range, the contours of the beach and jetty came slowly into view under the night sky. I roused the engine from its sleep of three days, pulled the throttle back long enough to throw a stiff shot of diesel down its throat, and heard it cough to life. Sails dropped to the deck. Lining up on the channel, which was dug wide and deep to allow cruise ships to come and go daily, I was soon steaming into the port that had so long been the object of my dreams.

Caught up as I was in the moment and thinking myself every inch of Balboa, my reverie ended abruptly when I nearly collided at flank speed with an unlit concrete piling. Swinging the boat's helm around at the last moment in a sudden and ungainly yaw, I narrowly escaped my just comeuppance. I could hardly complain of the hazard: I had drifted well outside the marked channel. Thus was I again reminded that a sailor's greatest peril is not a dragon of the deep but the places where little children go a-wading. Duly chastened, I skittered back into the channel and fixed my gaze tightly on the red and green lights ahead.

Chapter 39

LANDFALL NASSAU

Nassau's advantages as a natural harbor are unique in this region of the world. The name "Bahama" is a contraction of the Spanish phrase *"baja mar,"* which means "shallow sea." Unlike other ports of the Bahamas, which are rimmed by limestone banks and accessible only through narrow, shoaling inlets, the entrance to Nassau benefits from a wide natural lagoon that opens directly to deep water and is protected by a barrier island.

Nassau's charms were first and best appreciated by hordes of pirates—the infamous Blackbeard among them—who infested that port in the early 1700s. Today, a statue of Englishman Woodes Rogers, Nassau's colonial governor, stands at the entrance to the British Colonial Hilton hotel in the city. The inscription recalls his singular achievement: "Piracy expelled, commerce restored." More's the pity, if you ask me.

Nassau is indeed a commercial city. However, much of its infrastructure has been in decline since the 1970s, when the island gained independence from the British government. Some roads are in awful shape. There is no significant farming or manufacturing anywhere on the island, and the major export—fish—accounts for only a small percentage of the population's gross domestic product. The soil is poor, and as a result the island imports eighty percent of its food. The local economy depends heavily on offshore banking, tourism from cruise ships, and foreign-owned resorts and casinos.

The Atlantis resort is the city's major private employer. Here I found well-heeled tourists willing to blow hundreds of dollars a night on a hotel room and hundreds more in the casino, all the while enjoying a Disney World send-up of Bahamian life that bears little resemblance to the surrounding reality.

Still, everywhere around Nassau the natural beauty of the island and its culture breaks through the concrete and commercialism. Coconut palms sway overhead, flowers bloom in every crevice, and the aroma of fish and mango roasting on Arawak Cay travels on the ever-present breeze. Even in the shallowest, most obscure corner, amid grubby workboats, the water of the harbor is still as clear as a Beverly Hills swimming pool. The most remarkable gem to be found on this island, however, is its people. The King's English is spoken here, and as I would learn in traveling the breadth and length of New Providence over the next eight months, the quaintly formal British manner, imbued with strong native pride, is everywhere in evidence.

It was nine o'clock in the evening on Sunday, April 4, 2010, when the *Gypsy Moon* arrived at the anchorage in Nassau Harbor. The area reserved for transient boats lies just west of the two high-span bridges that arch over the harbor between East Bay Street and Paradise Island. Of the several boats at anchor, none had lights on below to indicate that a crew was aboard. Circling twice to find a spot with adequate swinging room, I noticed that depths in the anchorage shoaled quickly to six feet. A half-submerged derelict near shore warned me to stay well out in the harbor, which I was only too happy to do.

Gypsy Moon's plow anchor dropped with a splash from her bow, and forty feet of chain and rode paid out slowly in the gentle evening breeze. I tested the holding ground with the engine under reverse power, watching the lights onshore to be certain I wasn't dragging anchor, then throttled down to full engine stop.

All was quiet. I felt the singular joy of having come a great distance under sail that at the outset had seemed unimaginable and impassable. I had made good on a promise to myself. I had done the thing I'd said I would do, and that meant much more to me than it likely meant to anyone who'd heard me say it. Mercifully, I had sailed this final leg under a benevolent star, such that my voyage was without storms, equipment failures, or errors of navigation or seamanship. It had all gone so remarkably well and quickly.

In my mind's eye, the docks at Annapolis were as clear as those I could see behind me. I recalled with a satisfied nostalgia the mixed feelings of dread, anticipation, and uncertainty I had felt when departing from that city's harbor one thousand miles and eight months ago.

From my view on deck, the now brightly lit towers of Atlantis were prominent against the night sky and gave an air of enchantment to the place where I had just arrived. This was no banana backwater, I thought. This was Neptune's playground. I tidied up the sails that I had furled in haste before coming through the channel and then organized the general clutter below from the previous days spent living at a steep angle of heel. Before long, all was well aboard my tiny spaceship on Planet Nassau, and I was deeply asleep.

Chapter 40

COMING ASHORE

On my first morning in paradise, I slept in. I am one of the rare few who find the vee berth of the *Gypsy Moon* spacious and comfortable. I was content to wait for the Bahamian sunshine to spill through the hatch and wake me. It had been a welcome comfort, that first night at anchor, not to have to pop my head through the companionway every hour to look for the odd marauding supertanker that might be bearing down upon my little boat.

Nassau Harbor on that Monday morning was bustling with activity. The mail boat was in, and everywhere little skiffs that tended fish shacks at Potter's Cay were coming and going. Potter's Cay has been for centuries and is today the place where native Bahamians come to buy and eat fresh fish from colorfully painted shanties and to send and receive goods carried among the outer islands aboard cargo boats.

My first order of business was to secure a suitable berth where I could leave the boat before returning to the United States by air. Before arriving, I had chosen the Nassau Yacht Haven as a home for *Gypsy Moon* through the coming hurricane season. Once the anchor was up that Monday morning and the engine was purring, I returned to my easterly heading in the channel to find this marina.

It was not as easy as all that. Like most places in the islands, the marina didn't advertise itself with a flashy entrance as most American marinas do. It was tucked in behind rows of wooden docks and a fuel pier in the "working" end of Nassau Harbor. I radioed the dockmaster about my impending arrival, and he answered promptly. A fellow named Sidney appeared on the outer dock, caught my line, and showed great concern in selecting the best slip for a long-term stay. For the next thirty minutes, I put Sidney through some needless calisthenics to determine why the shore power at my new slip wasn't working, only to discover that the boat's circuit breaker had tripped back in Port Canaveral. Sidney responded with a weary smile that told me I wasn't his first idiot that week and would probably not be his last.

With the push of a button the circuits were electrified, and the *Gypsy Moon* again became a home of modern convenience, now in the exotic port of Nassau. With difficulty, I resisted the impulse to dress ship and call the embassy to invite the ambassador aboard for dinner.

Walking onto the pier at the Nassau Yacht Haven wasn't even one small step for mankind, but it was a giant leap for me. I had come here first by plane the year before, when I began considering a solo voyage, to look for a place to tuck the *Gypsy Moon* in for a long summer's nap. It had taken navigating airport security, long flights and connections, baggage hassles, cabs, a hotel, and no small sum of money to reach the island back then. Looking down from thirty thousand feet, it seemed daunting that I should attempt to travel at four knots the same distance it was taking me several hours to span at jet speeds.

To be honest, I never thought I would make it. Even when I had stood on this same pier all those months ago, assuring the dock-master that I would be pleased to rent a slip, I felt very much the poser. I feared this voyage to Nassau was just a pipe dream of mine that was destined to fade away for some reason or another, as most dreams do.

Now, standing in the hot Bahamian sun, I frankly did not recognize the confident fellow who nonchalantly stepped off my boat onto the streets of Nassau as though he made such voyages all the time. If I was fooling anyone by my bravado (not likely), I certainly wasn't fooling myself. In my wildest imagination I might have been Charles Lindbergh in Paris, but in my heart I was just a kid who had taken his tricycle around the block for the first time and was astonished not to have met the bogeyman along the way.

Concluding the particulars of my slip rental at the harbormaster's office, I inquired about a bus to Christ Church. My flight was scheduled to leave that evening, and I didn't have much time. Soon enough, I was aboard one of the many small buses that ferry passengers around the city for about $1.50. They are a mainstay of the local population and a great way to get to know ordinary Bahamians.

Riding the bus on this and many other occasions, I saw young children traveling to and from school unfailingly greet the driver and those on board with a respectful "Good morning" or "Good afternoon." They wore school uniforms that were clean, starched, and pressed. Their demeanor was cheerful and polite, and they spoke in complete, intelligible sentences to elders and strangers. No one was walking about in his underwear with his pants at his knees. No one was tattooed, pierced, or spiked. People made eye contact and smiled.

I am not ignorant of the high rate of drug-related crimes in Nassau, and it is impossible not to notice the relative poverty that exists in places in the city. However, speaking only from my own experience, I saw very little antisocial behavior of any kind. In fact, over the nine months I spent there I regularly encountered the most scrupulous manners from people at every echelon of that society. While I wouldn't wish for their economy, we may well need to discover their secrets of elementary education and apply them in the United States.

At last, I arrived on foot at the stately stone cathedral of Christ Church, which has stood at the corner of George and King Streets since the year 1670. It was the Tuesday after Easter, and the pastor was on vacation. Apparently that is the custom after the rigors of Holy Week and the many responsibilities of that high season to which the clergy must attend. Thus, after a thousand miles of ocean I was unable personally to deliver my tiny cargo to the assistant pastor to whom I had promised the gift in a letter written the previous fall.

With my arrival rather late and unannounced as it was, I was certainly not perturbed at the reverend's absence. I was pleased instead to present the book to the church secretary. Dimly recalling my letter of months before, she received my unscheduled visit with aplomb—even posing for a picture in the sanctuary while holding the book I had the honor to inscribe with a message of goodwill. This photo was duly presented to the pastor in Raleigh, and thus was the Queen Isabella of my journey given her due.

Within a few hours of delivering my gift to the church, I was airborne again, retracing the slow voyage of the *Gypsy Moon* at speeds unknown to nature and the Great Age of Sail. While I was glad for the means that modern industry and the ingenuity of man had afforded me to return so quickly to hearth and home, I was gladder still to have made the outbound journey slowly, with time for reflection and understanding. One can travel a thousand miles in a matter of hours today and experience nothing. But the voyage I had just completed could not be measured in a span of distance or time. I had ventured inward to an uncharted place, found no dragons, and returned to tell the tale. Clouds of self-doubt were beginning to part in the brilliant Caribbean sky. Where the voyage was headed I did not know, but where it had taken me so far had already changed my life forever.

LATITUDE 21.76.48 N
LONGITUDE 72.17.45 W
PROVIDENCIALES, TURKS AND
CAICOS ISLANDS

Chapter 41

SAILORS AND LUNATICS

This voyage did not begin, back in August 2009, with the idea that it would change my life or anyone else's. Seeing no better plan, I had cast my fate to the wind; but the wind being the fickle fellow he is, I expected nothing more from this gesture in the end than I would from a helium balloon that escapes a child's hand. The thrill and wonder of its sudden rise belies the quiet ignominy of its inevitable, unseen descent.

Yet what I came to see in my little vessel, as she completed each successive leg of the voyage, bloodied but unbowed, was a realization of what we were both stubbornly capable of achieving. I began to kindle a hope, and soon that hope became a plan, that I might actually *keep going.*

Let there be no mistake: there is madness in any attempt at a voyage around the world in a small boat. I have known sailors all my life, and I am here to tell you that no one who seeks such an adventure is in his right mind, nor has anyone in his right mind ever completed the task. To the willing fool it offers scorching sun, sudden storms, poor food, scarce water, sleepless nights, and lonely days, among other petty discomforts and mortal dangers.

Hollywood, the artist's canvas, and the printed page have yet to capture the stark reality of the unforgiving sea. Ages before Darwin, the writer of Genesis revealed the ocean to be the origin of species with the words, "And God said, Let the waters bring forth abundantly the moving creature that hath life...." Yet for all its teeming vitality, the sea is a billowing desert to mortal man. He cannot live long in it or upon it. The faith of Peter could not traverse it, and not for nothing did the disciples wake Jesus to quell its rage. Its watery depths wait ever ready for the careless step or the failing grasp that in an instant can turn a sailor's bright, sun-kissed afternoon into the twilight of his eternal repose.

But sane or not, each man has only his own heart to guide him—not those of his wiser friends. If he has a deep yearning to go, he is not likely to find any greater peace in the resistance of that desire. The only thing left is for him to sail and to keep sailing until he either comes to his senses, comes all the way around to the place where he began, or sinks somewhere in between. By just such a course was the New World discovered by a small group of terrified Italians. By this same haphazard route must every man find his own destiny, using whatever vessel his life may offer. All of us, before the end, must find our way to some unseen shore, however distant, and there plant the flag that will stand as testament to the reason why we made the voyage.

I am accustomed to being asked by strangers, well-meaning friends, and family whether I am afraid that I might encounter storms, fall overboard, be set upon by bloodthirsty pirates, or suffer some life-threatening illness in the middle of the ocean, far from aid. When they bring up these wild imaginings, I first reassure them that my days at sea are not nearly so cinematic. Yes, there is a risk in ocean voyaging. The boat has not been built nor the man born to sail her who can survive every storm. But dangerous storms come and go according to a predictable calendar in most parts of the world. What can be predicted can be avoided, and what cannot be avoided cannot be helped. A careful man and a well-found boat are both safe at sea, and to cross oceans is hardly to test the Lord's mercy in the way some do by jumping out of airplanes, smoking cigarettes, or running with the bulls at Pamplona.

It is wrongheaded, in my view, to imagine that life is lived on a linear plane somewhere between opposite poles of risk and reward. There is another dimension. Even the most sober, sane, and cautious life is temporary. What makes for a life well lived is not the length of our days but how we spend them. Never sail an ocean and you will surely never die at sea, but die you surely will. We cannot stack that deck or cheat the dealer. Yet we Americans in particular strive mightily to do so.

Much has been written about our youth-oriented culture, and that phenomenon is easy enough to understand. Who wouldn't prefer to be young and attractive and vital? But less is understood about the flip side of our preoccupation with youth, which is an irrational fear of death. We seem to regard death not as the inevitable end of all things, but as a kind of grand larceny of our basic human rights. Our uniquely American lust for justice will not be served until the root causes of this heinous crime, be they the failures of our medical or political or economic systems, are legislated and litigated into oblivion. This is the great folly of our time.

Like the bloom of a rose, the beauty of all life is organic and, therefore, limited by time. Look around you. Most of the people you see will have left this earth in fifty short years, and the rest will be crowding the exits. Yet knowing this, when we hear the story of a man and woman who are lost at sea or killed by Somali pirates while living out their dream to sail the world, some of us privately congratulate ourselves for having the good sense to stay home. We see their deaths and shudder, but were we able to foresee our own deaths, would we feel so smug about our choices versus theirs? Isn't it really our manner of living that matters most, not our manner of dying?

It is an article of popular faith that if only we eat our vegetables, recycle, and exercise regularly, we can somehow arrange to meet Death on our own terms, peaceably in our sleep. Such nonsense. Death is not a peaceable fellow, no matter where he does his work. But Life is different. She is a fickle beauty to be relentlessly wined and dined, and no man stands a chance of winning her heart unless he is willing to risk losing her forever.

Our irrational hope that Death will come for thee but not for me drives the nation's politics, the world's economy, and many of the choices of our daily lives. We plan for the future as though we will live forever, yet we worry incessantly about pensions, health insurance, and jobs. We protest that our leaders aren't doing more to address the crisis of our dependence on these castles of sand. For the vast majority of us, however, this anxiety cannot be explained by any reasonable fear that we will ever be hungry or lack the basic comforts of life, many of which are beyond the imagination of millions of people in the Third World. For many of us life is rich to the point of gluttony, and that overconsumption more than anything else is what threatens our longevity.

So to my worried family and friends clinging tightly to this life, who see sailing upon the open ocean as a reckless risk of all that I should hold dear, I lovingly demur. The world offers no safe harbor—that is an illusion. The end comes for us all, and if we choose to remain in port, it will come for us there. I for one am in no hurry to rush out to meet it, but neither do I see the point of altering my course in fear of its arrival. It is life that I am at risk of meeting on the open sea—not Death, who already knows where to find me.

Chapter 42

A Pilgrim's Tale

I have a story to tell you of Nassau. In our shrinking world you hardly have need of my memoir to know something of that story already. Millions come here aboard cruise ships and airplanes, just as hordes now span in a matter of hours all the hard-won miles of Magellan's passage to the Philippines. But what I have to report is something that might have escaped the harried traveler's eye.

In the months over the summer and fall of 2010, Susan and I came by air to the island for a week or two at a time to tend to the *Gypsy Moon* during her layover. Through the wonders of the Internet, I was able to continue my work there as easily as if I had been sitting in my office chair. And when I was not working, I had the privilege of waking up aboard a small boat, just a few feet from the waterline in the harbor, with absolutely nothing to do. I held this important agenda in common with assorted geckos, crabs, and the odd damselfish. With my fair complexion and blue eyes I would never be mistaken for a native, but I had the privilege of lollygagging around town in a way that only a native could afford.

It bears repeating that many of the people I encountered in Nassau and throughout the Bahamas, most without emblems of material wealth or social status, had a conspicuous refinement of manners and a genuine way of kindness. I met one such man on a Sunday morning at Christ Church.

Susan and I usually made an effort to attend services whenever we were on the island. The organist at the cathedral had such a talent as to summon the angels to Earth with every chorus, and had I not even a mustard seed of faith I would have come to that pew just for the music.

On Sunday mornings, Susan would glide out of the marina shower room, smartly dressed in a skirt and sandals, her long blond hair catching the sunlight, looking as if she were headed to a summer fashion show at the British Colonial Hilton. I, on the other hand, in the rumpled sport coat, threadbare trousers, and wrinkled tie I kept aboard the boat, was impervious to the improvements of fashion. Walking with Susan through town on our way to church, I looked like a homeless man stalking a beautiful woman.

Those familiar with the Episcopal liturgy know that its various passages and prayers are hopscotched about in different parts of three sources, these being the Book of Common Prayer, the hymnal, and the missalette that is handed to you at the door. (The number three is important here because it is exactly one more than the number of hands you have.) Before the unwitting visitor has had time to rehearse his steps, the reading of the Mass begins like a heavenly quadrille. The priest at the altar calls the count, and the faithful whirl smartly from one text to the next, in unison and on cue. Rarely are these holy mysteries revealed to the uninitiated by something as banal as a page number announced in advance, out loud, with time given to arrive there before the entire assembly has darted away into yet another secret passage of the Mass, like a school of fish pursued by a shark.

Adding to the complexity of this ritual is the need to rise, sit, or kneel at appointed times, not unlike a game of musical chairs. Thus are the interloper and the infidel revealed—standing rod straight and suddenly alone in the middle of the seated assembly, holding two books while dropping another, thumbing anxiously for the correct page, and running frantically to join the group at the boarding gate but arriving just after the last prayer has left the terminal.

Susan and I found ourselves in this unfortunate condition one morning during Sunday Mass at Christ Church. The cathedral is part of the Anglican Communion, which is the name given to the Church of England in countries outside the United States. Owing to its geography, the Bahamian church has acquired some liturgical oddities uncommon to its American counterpart. We found ourselves anxiously thumbing and flipping and stumbling to follow along that day.

A Bahamian man standing alone a great distance away in the row ahead of us must have noticed our confusion. He calmly walked the length of his empty pew and, leaning toward us, demonstrated the correct page of the text. He waited until we had rejoined the throng and then, smiling in response to our expression of thanks, returned to his distant place in the pew.

On that Sunday in Nassau, the same man found it necessary to rescue and redirect us on three more occasions before the Mass was through. Each time he did so, I marveled at his ability to know the very instant at which we had lost our way, despite my effort to mumble something suitably devotional and otherworldly. Where others might merely have averted their eyes to save us any embarrassment as we muddled through, this man conspicuously offered assistance when it was needed.

It's a simple thing, you might say, to help a fellow parishioner find his place in the prayer book, and it is something I am sure occurs in churches across the world every Sunday. Three things, however, were unusually endearing about this man.

First, he was not seated in the same pew as Susan and me, where it would hardly discomfit anyone to offer assistance if it were needed and could easily be given. I have been in churches my whole life, and never have I been concerned about anyone's need for guidance from fifteen feet away, much less suffered the Lord the interruption of my own important prayers to aid another soul in his.

Secondly, this man was not at all concerned about intruding upon the pageantry of the moment or our pretension to be a part of it, which is no small portion of the Episcopalian experience. That would have counseled against drawing attention to us in any way. But this was no taciturn High Church patrician. This man wanted to ensure that we received the full measure of that for which we had come, which was a meaningful communion with the Almighty. Each time he walked over to us, I had the distinct feeling that Susan and I were straggling sheep who had caught the shepherd's watchful eye and that the shepherd was gently guiding us back into the fold.

The man was not a member of the church vestry, hoping to endear himself to us and to endear us in turn to the annual capital campaign. Hale and hearty, he appeared to be in his thirties. He held no office in the church that I could discern. His plain clothes, in contrast to the fastidious attire of even the poor who attend church in Nassau, suggested to me that he was poorer than most. There was no air of pridefulness in his commendable piety.

This is but one example of many small kindnesses we observed in our travels around Nassau, and it is a memorable one. Although we were the strangers that day in the cathedral, the experience recalled for me the apostle's promise that in those whom we encounter in this life, we sometimes meet "angels unawares."

A Pilgrim's Tale

I hope my Episcopal friends will take no offense at this admittedly exaggerated bit of fun-poking at our famously formal and erudite tradition. I am foremost among the lovers of old stone cathedrals and the old stone people who fill them every Sunday. After a twenty-year sojourn in the post–Vatican II equanimity of the Catholic Mass, where the pipe organ has been replaced by besandaled guitar players and every hymn seems to be just another formless variation of the same Peter, Paul and Mary tune, I found myself . pining for the pomp and circumstance of the Episcopal liturgy and a rousing chorus of "A Mighty Fortress Is Our God." And having now by turns managed to offend Catholics everywhere, let me repair further by acknowledging what the world already knows, which is that there is nowhere to be found a greater benefactor of the poor and downtrodden than the Catholic Church, and it is after all by our good works—not choirs or Sunday pageantry—that our faith is proved.

Chapter 43

GOLDEN CALVES

New Providence Island is well traveled and has been for centuries, but it held for me a few notable first impressions that I will attempt here to describe along with some advice to any who might follow in my wake. (You may have guessed from the title of this chapter that I am not quite done railing against the evils of wealth and greed. If you will forgive me this further brief sermon, I promise we will soon set sail again.)

I suggest that in Nassau you avoid the casinos, which you will find not only here but everywhere in the Caribbean. No doubt I am excessively Victorian about the whole matter, but they seem mostly to serve vacationing Americans who have so lost their sense of what really matters in life that they have come to believe they can find it at the bottom of a slot machine, and they pay dearly every night to be proven wrong.

Susan and I often traveled on foot between our marina and the sprawling resort of Atlantis, where, after a certain hour in the evening, we could tour the capacious underground aquarium known as the Dig at no charge. (The glass tunnel through a colony

of spiny lobsters was an especially creepy thrill.) Once within the resort, we could obtain, for the price of a tot of rum, a table in one of
the hotel bars from which to enjoy a live band. Getting around the
resort for these miserly entertainments, though, required us to traverse the long, dark hall of the Atlantis casino.

I have nothing against gambling per se. In fact, I have always considered the chance to see Thoroughbred racehorses run a form of
entertainment well worth the price of a losing wager, within reason. Part of the mythology surrounding my father's life, before he
descended into alcoholism, is that he wrote a thesis in statistics at
Columbia on his theory for picking winning horses at the track. I
have his degree from that institution hanging on my wall, so presumably he received a passing grade on the paper, but my family can
attest that his formula had serious flaws in its practical application.

Far removed from the romance of Churchill Downs, casinos
evoke (for me, at least) a gauche pseudoelegance that mocks the sophistication they strive so hard to convey—something like Saddam
Hussein's gilded royal toilet. I found the casino in Atlantis thick with
cigarette smoke and an air of despair, full of depressed middle-aged
tourists hypnotized late into the evening by blinking colored lights
and ringing bells. Incredibly, they could not see that their salvation
lay just yards away on a beautiful moonlit beach.

Another peculiarity one soon recognizes when traveling the
Caribbean is the number of megayachts in the harbors. I'm not
talking about a few big boats. I'm talking about a lot of really big
boats—private ships, in fact, manned by their own full-time cap-
tains, crew, and staff, all smartly turned out in uniform. You will
see them pulled alongside the docks in Atlantis and other ultra-
deluxe resorts, where the owners pay gladly for use of the long piers
needed to accommodate these leviathans.

I made a point of chatting up some of the crew of these ships when I spotted them coming or going on deck as I walked around the marina. There is a whole subculture of people who make a living moving from place to place and ship to ship, serving as cooks or crew. I was glad not to be one of them. The sheer size of these vessels affects me with a kind of inverse claustrophobia.

You might as well tie a man to a tree as put him in such a boat. The lure of the sea is its promise of a carefree, adventurous, and romantic life, however illusory that promise may turn out to be for some. Yet there is nothing carefree about a vessel that consumes more diesel fuel in an hour than a sailboat will burn in a decade. The man who buys that boat with dreams of a life of unfettered ease in the warm tropical sunshine is headed for a rude awakening, unless he is traveling with the Sultan of Brunei. This is why many of the great luxury motor yachts that you see steaming around Nassau and other harbors throughout the world will appear sooner than you think in the pages of *Yachting* magazine, offered for sale at an enormous loss by older and wiser men to younger and more foolish ones.

For all the glitz that has become of Robinson Crusoe's island home, somewhere at this hour in the Caribbean there is a man on a small boat with well-worn sails, secure in an anchorage he has purchased only by the wind and the grace it took to get there, preparing to enjoy for the price of a little rice, a few vegetables, and a fish willing to be fooled, a meal fit for a king served at the best table in the house.

I would love to be able to tell you that I have embodied or at least aspired to that lone sailor's way of life, never succumbing to the siren song of wealth and conspicuous consumption. But if you have known any part of my story, you know there would be nothing but vanity in such a boast.

My house would be a castle in the sky to the average Dominican child, and my boat might as well be a spaceship to a man in Haiti. I write these very words from the comfort of a gleaming, climate-controlled office tower on dry land. It has been five months since I have seen the *Gypsy Moon*, and two more months will pass before I can return to her.

Too rarely do I have the strength of my own convictions, and whatever wisdom there may be in my words, it is too slowly proved by my actions. I more often aspire to the ideals of Vanderbilt than St. Vincent, and I am more prone to hubris than humility. But hope springs eternal for the prodigal's return.

Look for him at sundown on the wane of an east wind, carried gently by the tide to a quiet cove where there is sand firm enough to hold an anchor and mountains high enough to provide shelter. There if indeed he is blessed will he come, penniless, to the royal manor that has been prepared for him. Within it he will find a feast to give strength to the weary, the peace that passes all understanding, and riches untold.

Chapter 44

WHAT THE NOMAD KNOWS

Nassau was unscathed by hurricanes in the summer and fall of 2010. Once the threat of tropical storms had faded, I made preparations to sail again. The days after Christmas would afford the first opportunity. Susan thought to accompany me, but in sailing around New Providence Island over the summer, she had shown a propensity toward seasickness. We thought it best that she wait for a shorter passage to discover whether those symptoms might be persistent.

During a period of up to two weeks, I intended first to head east, well out into deep water, and then south as far as I could go, wind and weather permitting. Past experience had taught me not to promise or plan where I might land. Instead, I loaded enough food and water for a month and hoped to find a friendly landfall in no more than half that time.

There is a great deal written about preferred passages in the Bahamas. As was the case with the crossing of the Gulf Stream at Florida, all manner of disaster is predicted for those who do not follow the conventional wisdom. Most boats heading south from

Nassau opt to travel a protected route over the Bahama Banks behind Eleuthera and Cat Islands. Eventually they follow other boats into Georgetown on Long Island, which I am told has acquired, over the years, the nickname Chicken Harbor. The name owes its origin to the fact that the passage south from Georgetown is across open water, and apparently many boaters never summon the courage to attempt it, choosing instead to return north.

The great majority of sailboats making passages anywhere in the Bahamas do so in a series of day trips, mostly under power rather than under sail, anchoring nightly along the way. This practice is explained by the fact that the shallow banks require navigation by sight to avoid unmarked shoals. The relative scarcity of good anchorages and the necessity to make it to one before dark each day require a kind of planning that the vagaries of wind and weather rarely afford. So the next time a friend tells you he is "sailing" in the Bahamas, understand that he is either going in circles or mostly motoring during daylight from harbor to harbor. The *Gypsy Moon* would, by necessity as well as the preference of her captain, take a different tack.

I arrived in Nassau on the afternoon of New Year's Day. From the airport, my taxi took me through downtown on East Bay Street, where the viewing stands for the annual Junkanoo celebration were still in place. I was sorry to have missed that party but glad to have spent New Year's Eve in Raleigh, where I could kiss my wife at midnight before embarking on another long passage alone.

I settled up and left the docks at Nassau Yacht Haven on the morning of January 2, 2011. Owing to the unexpected swiftness of the tide, my departure was an unseamanlike affair, aided greatly (again) by Sidney standing on the dock, maneuvering two stern lines like the reins of a show pony. For my part, I was running fore and aft on deck in a disorderly panic, using a long pole to fend off docks, pilings, and other boats, as if the *Gypsy Moon* were being attacked from all sides by a pack of wild dogs. All of 11,700 pounds and equipped with only a single-propeller twenty-horsepower engine, my boat was built for sailing, not maneuvering in tight places under power. She backs out of a marina slip with all the grace of a pig in a poke. I usually pull her out by hand, using lines. This day, however, the tide was too strong and had the best of all of us, which is perfectly why it is said that the tide waits for no one.

Finally, this circus trapeze act succeeded in getting the *Gypsy*'s nose pointed east, and I headed out from the marina to the channel—my feathers slightly ruffled but still in place. No doubt the lunch crowd overlooking the marina from the Poop Deck restaurant wondered why this unpracticed helmsman was taking a vessel out to sea, and I was doing my best to shrug off the same doubts.

I rounded the jetty where the lighthouse stands at the entrance to Nassau Harbor and, against the easterly trades, took a bearing for north by northeast. I had sixty miles to go to get to the passage between Great Abaco and Eleuthera Islands, after which I would tack south on a heading that would keep me in deep water, well clear of land. Once I made this turn, I would be exposed to three thousand miles of uninterrupted swell in the Atlantic Ocean as it sweeps westward from the Cape Verde Islands, off the coast of Africa. That thrilling prospect is the source of such fear and trepidation in the sailing community that few boats take this course. It was not surprising, then, that after midafternoon of the second day, I saw no other boats for four days.

The offshore, easterly trade winds are regular and strong, and I was happy to depend on them as I pushed southward. I found that my desired heading placed the *Gypsy Moon* on a broad reach—her most favored attitude—which made her exceptionally easy to balance for self-steering. Suddenly, I had very little to do but contemplate the fact that in a few days' time, I would share with Columbus the experience of seeing the island of San Salvador rise slowly from the Atlantic.

I occupied much of my free time reading *The Sacred Journey* by Charles Foster. Foster is an Oxford fellow who makes a persuasive case, to which I ascribe, that since the time of Cain and Abel, God has had a soft spot in His heart for nomads of all kinds and is most vividly present in their midst. Though it is not a book about sailing per se, its theme that revelation comes to those who journey along the world's lonely roads applies equally to nomads of the sea.

The old Shaker hymn rightly observes that simplicity is a gift. Wealth and success often rob us of that gift. By necessity, however, those who take the road less traveled must travel light. What the nomad richly receives when he tears down the scaffolding of civilization is a better appreciation for the bulwarks of faith. Foster's book on this subject was as welcome as an old friend on my own journey, and I returned to it again and again to continue the conversation. I was sorry to come to the end.

Speaking of gifts, I also had occasion on these days spent coasting out to sea far from land, along the length of Eleuthera and Cat Islands, to take stock of my own good fortune. As I stared upward for long hours from the pilot berth, it dawned upon me that I was, against all odds, a happily married man. I had just celebrated the first anniversary of my encounter with the Siren of Charleston. With her I had found a depth of love and intimacy that I had not thought possible, but that was not the only change of the past year. My life at home and at work had been thoroughly transformed.

Susan had brought her considerable skills as an accountant to my law practice and freed me from the bondage of billing and paying bills. I became a better and more successful lawyer as a result. My tiny practice was humming along, with a growing staff over which

Susan hovered with the devotion of a mother hen. At home, clean underwear began to appear in my dresser drawer, neatly folded and sorted, as if by magic. For my part, I strove to ensure that Susan never prepared a single meal, washed a dish, or made a single trip to the grocery store. I found new meaning in simple acts of service, and I reveled in Susan's approval of my culinary efforts, intramural though they were.

Now, coming upon two years together as I write these words, it occurs to me that the secret of our happiness—apart from the love that every successful marriage requires—is time. With rare exception, the table is set each morning for breakfast, often with flowers from our garden, and time is deliberately taken to enjoy that meal together. Each night, dinner is served by candlelight, with time for conversation. We dance everywhere, sleep in, play and tease constantly, and make love in the morning long after we should be getting ready for work.

We sometimes fight like children, but we make up like lovers, and we help each other remember the need we each have to forgive and be forgiven. Living without television, we have taken back whole months of our lives that would otherwise have been lost to the time-sink of sitcoms, reality shows, and political screaming matches. We take the time to read the paper together each morning. Banana pancakes and French toast are weekly staples. We cherish slow walks through the farmers' market and lazy Sunday afternoons at home, when Susan fusses about the yard, I make meals for the week, and both of us stop to dance to tunes from *A Prairie Home Companion* coming from the clock radio in the kitchen.

We revel in the holidays and throw messy get-togethers for neighbors and friends. We have rediscovered the lost tradition of the dinner party, but we more often spend quiet nights together, just the two of us, watching classic old movies (for me) and syrupy romantic comedies (for her). In short, we devote ourselves to each other as best we know how and promise to keep going, no matter what. We also regularly find our way to church, where I feel compelled to express, along with my thanks, my incredulity at having been blessed so greatly in excess of anything I deserve.

All of this sounds terribly Pollyanna even to me, as one who knows it to be true. I don't mean to make a caricature of our marriage or marriage in general. Susan and I live as others do, in the real world and not in a fairy tale. She is a woman through and through, and I am a man, with a man's usual flaws. No man or woman married more than a month needs to read an essay of mine to understand the stubborn differences between men and women. Like life itself, marriage is not always easy, but it is always worth it. And through it all, I have scarcely been able to take my eyes off her. She remains the most beautiful and genuine woman who has ever given me the time of day, and the clock still stops for me when she walks into a room.

Chapter 45

JOURNEY OF THE MAGI

I *have wondered* at times whether the whole idea of crossing oceans in a small boat isn't evidence of a tendency toward delusions of grandeur. If that be so, there can be few delusions as grand as to compare such a voyage to the journey of the wise men who followed a star to the manger at Bethlehem.

The church's liturgical calendar compels us to contemplate the sacred mystery of the Christ child each December, and during my contemplation of the impending passage south from Nassau, it occurred to me that I would be arriving somewhere—I had no idea where—around the Feast of the Epiphany. It seemed the perfect excuse to come bearing gifts.

I have had this delusion once before. In 1991, while I was still in Houston, some friends and I formed the Magi Foundation—a Texas nonprofit whose sole purpose was to raise money to purchase Christmas gifts to be delivered aboard sailboats to poor children during an annual offshore regatta from Galveston to Corpus Christi. Five boats entered that year and were loaded with several thousand dollars' worth of new toys. They set sail the day after Thanksgiving, but only one boat made it through a squall that produced fifty-knot gusts and fifteen-foot seas. (That storm remains the only occasion when I have been sick at sea, and I was as sick as a dog.) The boats turned back by the storm put in at Port O'Connor, and the toys they carried were delivered to Catholic Charities in Corpus Christi by "another way" (airplane) that recalled the biblical course change given to the three wise men in a dream.

Nineteen years later, to the delight of a passel of Sunday school children of St. Michael's Episcopal Church in Raleigh and their long-suffering teachers, I agreed to carry aboard the *Gypsy Moon* a bundle filled with their homemade Christmas cards, a video greeting, and other gifts to the unseen children of the unknown island where I might land. As it had on the gulf shores of Texas in 1991, King Herod's ghost would again bode ill for my arrival.

It was the third day out from Nassau when I first saw the low green outline of the island of San Salvador. Thought to have been Columbus's first landfall in the New World, it could easily have been missed altogether. Unlike New Providence Island, from which I had just come, San Salvador is more sparsely populated and less densely developed today.

The wind was backing from the east to the southeast as I approached San Salvador, and tempted as I was to land there, the gorgeous weather gave me no reason to interrupt the steady flow of miles beneath my keel. I decided instead to leave the western shore of the island to port, wending my way through the channel that divides San Salvador from Rum Cay. As I did so, an enormous jetliner lifted off from the island, causing me to double-check my location in the chart book. The book revealed that I had not strayed off course and that San Salvador does indeed have a commercial airport. I smiled to imagine what might have been the effect on Columbus and his crew had this gleaming silver bird ascended from the island when they arrived there.

As night fell, I found myself on a direct course for Rum Cay. I was having a hard time making easting against the trades to get back into deep water, where I'd have plenty of sea room. The chart book spoke of a suitable marina and accommodations on Rum Cay, but there was no major airport for me to use in traveling back to the States, if I were to leave the boat there. I began to wonder if I should have stopped at San Salvador. Still, I had been out only three days, and I had a lot of time and good weather on my hands. I threw the helm over to port and made my way north by northeast again, toward the open ocean.

In the darkness, I had difficulty discerning my distance from the sparse lights on the south shore of San Salvador as I passed it, headed northeast. The boat wanted to head farther north than I would let her, and I was luffing sails as it was to stay on a course that would keep me off the lee shore. Trying to make the most out of every tack, I relied heavily on the depth sounder and GPS to tell me when I was approaching shallow water and needed to come about. It was a busy six hours of tacking maneuvers before I was far enough offshore again to resume a southeasterly heading.

By dawn of the fourth day, I was somewhere well east of Samana Cay, having sailed a distance of 350 miles since leaving Nassau in relatively light winds. Seas had been moderate and remained so.

Each day at three o'clock in the afternoon, I had a scheduled satellite phone call, first with Susan and then with others in my office before telling Susan good-bye for the day. The rented satellite phone was a welcome luxury and an extra margin of safety in the event of emergency. But unlike the cost to use land-based cellular phones, the cost of outgoing calls via satellite is still very dear. This brief daily conversation afforded me the opportunity to stay connected to Susan and put out any minor fires at the office. As I was far out of range of VHF weather forecasts at sea, these satellite phone calls were also my opportunity to learn details of the weather forecast for my position.

During the first four days of the trip, the weather had been so stable and mild that I did not bother to ask Susan for a forecast, and the weather on the fifth day was no different. For no apparent reason other than that I hadn't done so yet, I asked Susan on the fifth day to check what weather might lie ahead. I was very glad that she did.

Susan is not accustomed to wind speed forecasts, so it was with impressive nonchalance that she related the news that twenty-eight-to-thirty-one-knot winds were due to arrive just after eleven o'clock that night. The silence on the line when she said this attested to my dismay. I had been sailing for five days in winds of less than fifteen knots, under bluebird skies. I gently suggested that Susan recheck the numbers, but she had read the forecast correctly. Twenty-eight to thirty-one knots of wind would be blowing in six hours.

Sensing that she had said something unusual, Susan asked me what the matter was. With as much gratitude for the warning as genuine surprise, I told her that these wind speeds meant that I needed to go forward on deck, while it was still light outside, take down and stow all the long canvas I had flying, and dress the *Gypsy Moon* in her short knickers for heavy weather.

Once the sails were changed and her sail area had been reduced to a hankie-sized jib and trysail, the *Gypsy Moon*'s speed slowed to a lazy shuffle. She was moving not more than a knot or two per hour, and at this rate I would not be going anywhere soon. Still, if thirty-one-knot winds were about to hit, I knew that when they did I would be glad that I had raised the storm sails in advance.

Lying in the pilot bunk mostly wide awake, I watched the clock pass eleven that night, then twelve, one, two, and three in the morning, all the while the ocean was as calm as a sleeping baby. In my frustration, I wanted to call Susan and ask if she had not mistakenly read the weather forecast for El Salvador, a thousand miles away in Central America, instead of San Salvador, in the Bahamas. At four o'clock in the morning on a quiet sea the boat was still making very little headway, and I was kicking myself for not asking more questions about the forecast. I intended at first light to get a full complement of sails flying again.

When the clock struck five, as if on cue the wind started slowly increasing in intensity, like a man coming a long way to settle an old grudge. I was six days out, ten miles northeast of the island of Mayaguana, and at a point of decision whether to head southeast, toward Puerto Rico, or southwest, toward the Turks and Caicos. I was undecided on either course. Although the wind at that early hour was gaining strength and would clearly get stronger, the same forecast also called for winds and seas to drop on the seventh day and remain moderate for several days after that.

San Juan, Puerto Rico, was five hundred miles away from my position and at least a five-day sail. The island of Providenciales, or Provo, in the Turks and Caicos, was only thirty miles away. Puerto Rico sounded exciting, but I was tired. After a week alone at sea, I also missed my wife too much to choose a course that would require me to spend another week away from her, knowing that I had another option.

The chart book had pleasant things to say about Provo, but what drew me in was the description of the colonies of artists and craftsmen who populate the island and sell their creations in open markets. I had thought about one day opening a business for the export and sale of the handicrafts and jewelry I encountered in different countries along the voyage—something like privateering, but with a sales receipt. I took what I was reading and the occasion of this storm as reason enough to head south, not east, and make port at Provo.

What also caught my attention in the chart book, apart from the shopping advice about Provo, was the warning that anyone arriving at the island for the first time should employ a pilot to guide his boat through the serpentine maze of coral heads. One book recounted a horror story of a badly damaged boat and its stranded owners who ignored this advice. I didn't need to read that part twice.

Checking the information in the guide about Turtle Cove Marina, on the north shore of the island, I learned that it offered a pilot free of charge to arriving boats seeking dockage, but the pilot operated only until five o'clock in the afternoon and would travel only to the edge of the reef to meet an incoming boat. My position indicated that with a kick from the engine I could make it there in time.

The diesel engine rumbled to life, and I opened the throttle wide. The oil had just been changed in Nassau, only a month earlier, and I had run the engine less than forty-eight hours since that time. I had plenty of fuel. The small storm sails were doing more to steady the boat than drive her forward in the strong northwest wind, but with the added push of the diesel engine running at full throttle, the boat was soon making plenty of speed.

By six in the morning, the wind speed passed twenty knots. By ten o'clock, the wind hit its stride, and gusts were reaching thirty knots, judging from the sea state. By noon, the waves were up to ten feet and rising in large, foamy mounds above the stern as they raced the *Gypsy Moon* south. Old King Herod apparently did not like my new heading.

I have paid the price in the past for my lack of aptitude with diesel engines, and I paid the price again that day. When using the auxiliary only briefly to get in and out of a marina for weekend sailing back home, I could go an entire season and never need more than a cup of oil. Confident that my oil change less than a month earlier made it impossible that I could be low on oil from less than two full days of engine time, I failed to account for the fact that during those hours, the engine had run wide open and continuously. That meant it had reached and maintained an operating temperature that it doesn't usually see. That also explained why I was unaware it had burned so much oil that day on the open Atlantic.

At two in the afternoon, I was racing to meet the Turtle Cove Marina pilot before the twilight deadline. I had enough time to make it and would have done so easily if the engine had not suddenly throttled down to a stop. Never suspecting that I might be low on oil, I emptied one of the spare jerry cans of diesel strapped on deck into the fuel fill, thinking perhaps that at full throttle I had burned more fuel than usual and that the angle of heel was causing the fuel level on the cockpit gauge to read higher than it actually was. (It amazes me, in hindsight, how the human mind always prefers the most convenient explanation to the most logical one.)

I cranked the engine and got nothing. Next, I opened the primary filter in the fuel line to look for any algae or debris that might be causing a clog. It was as clean as a whistle, as was the secondary filter. Buttoning everything up and bleeding the fuel line of air as best I could, I cranked the engine again. It turned over but would give me nothing more.

Somewhere in the process of troubleshooting the engine, I used the satellite phone to contact folks at home in Raleigh, who in turn contacted local marinas until someone answered. A helpful British gentleman at one marina could offer no towing assistance but had a VHF radio with a range long enough to reach me. He hailed me on channel 16 and agreed to relay my coordinates to the Caicos Marina & Shipyard, which planned to send a boat out to that position, about ten miles away, and tow me through the reef. Reassured that help was on the way, I hove to the boat so she would come to a near stop and remain close to the position I had just reported, then went back to work on the engine.

Swearing disbelief that there could be any issue with the oil, I checked it just to be sure. The end of the dipstick was bone dry. I couldn't believe it. I added a full quart of oil before any level was visible, then more oil to bring it up to par. Still I got no response from the engine, and I knew that before long, repeated cranking of the electric starter would begin to take a toll on the battery. I could soon be out of power altogether.

I didn't have the good sense to give up right away. The English major in me is a little sensitive about my mechanical skill relative to other sailors, the vast majority of whom can fondly recall rebuilding the engine of their GTO in high school or some such thing. Although deep down I suspected that my efforts to revive the *Gypsy Moon*'s engine were making matters worse, not better, it was doing wonders for my self-esteem just to try.

Even drained batteries usually have enough of a second wind to start an engine if they are left alone awhile, and mine weren't drained yet. Suspecting that when I had checked the fuel filters I had introduced some air into the fuel line that was blocking the flow of diesel to the injectors, I gave the batteries a rest while I spent the next half hour massaging the manual fuel pump, looking for a bubble of air. I saw nothing but streams of fuel flowing down the side of the bleed screw. When the engine still wouldn't start after this effort, I knew I was out of options. Whatever the initial problem had been, it was now certifiably beyond my ability to diagnose or cure. There was nothing to do but maintain my position and keep a lookout for the towboat.

Although I was snug and safe under storm sails, as nightfall approached I began to doubt the reassurances being relayed to me from one marina through another on the VHF radio that a towboat was indeed underway for my position. Eventually it became apparent that, in the course of being passed from one radio to the next, the numerical coordinates of my position had been juxtaposed or misunderstood. I learned that the towboat had been searching for me for hours in another location, miles away. Just as the sun was setting, I received the unwelcome news that the tow operator had given up and that no help would arrive before morning.

I did consider for a moment the prospect of just sailing my way in, blind to the location of the reef, in hopes that I'd get lucky. The helpful Brit on the radio even made it sound easy and encouraged me to give it a try, which I knew meant that it was nigh impossible for mortal men and should not be attempted. Anxious though I was to reach the harbor, I eventually concluded that attempting to navigate the unmarked path through the coral heads at night under sail, under the effects of tide and current and without hope of aid from a working engine, would be more foolish than any mistake that had brought me to my present circumstance.

Never one to give up, my helpful British friend, who was still near enough to my position to reach me by radio, suggested that I sail fifteen miles south to an anchorage for the night at West Caicos Island, then sail fifteen miles back to meet the tow in the morning. I considered this as well. But looking at the chart for West Caicos Island and imagining the coral heads that might similarly complicate a landfall under sail there, I opted instead to heave to for the night in the safety of the open ocean. As namby-pamby as I'm sure that must have sounded to Mr. Churchill, I felt it was the right decision at the time. In one of the many ironies that seem to follow the *Gypsy*'s wake, I later learned that a sailboat overloaded with Haitian refugees wrecked on West Caicos Island just about the time of my arrival at Provo.

After tidying things up on deck and setting the initial heading on which the boat would be hove to for the next two-hour watch, I went below to boil some water for tea and make something comforting to eat. Before the kettle came to a boil, I noticed flashes of blue light coming through the cabin portholes. Running out on deck, I could hear the voices of several men in the darkness. Eventually I saw the dim outline of an approaching runabout. It was a police boat. The manager of the Caicos shipyard, true to his promise to send a tow for me that day, had arranged for a police boat to find me after the towboat operator had gone home.

I expressed my sincere gratitude that the men on the police boat had come to fetch me, after hours and this far out at sea. One asked if I had a towrope, which I did not. It was of some momentary concern to me that a boat had appeared to perform a tow without a proper towrope, but I quickly shrugged that off and went below to retrieve a spare halyard that could serve that purpose. Nylon halyards are long and strong but otherwise not ideal for towing, because they sink—a quality that would lead to an unexpected bit of fun later that night.

Before long the halyard was in place and ready for service. Now tethered to the *Gypsy Moon*, the police boat drifted away into the darkness. I could see very little other than a blue flashing light. I heard a voice ask for the draft of my boat, and I answered "Four feet two inches." "We should be fine, then" came the unseen reply. Hearing this remark, then seeing the police boat's initial heading on my GPS, I surmised that it was the driver's intention to cut across a corner of the reef and enter the channel from the side, rather than take the longer way around to enter the channel head-on from deep water. He must know the depth of the coral heads, I thought, and by asking for my draft merely wanted to confirm that my boat would pass safely above them. Local knowledge, after all, is what the prudent mariner is taught to prefer above all else—even printed nautical charts—when making navigational decisions. I didn't suppose that the knowledge in these parts could get any more local or reliable than a police boat.

It was a long way to the island. About a half hour after being given the assurance that "we should be fine," we were anything but.

Without warning, I felt the *Gypsy Moon* ride up sharply at the stern and careen to port, accompanied by a sickening, crunching sound, as if she'd been grabbed by the jaws of something beneath her. I was thrown off balance from my position behind the wheel when the boat abruptly stopped and leaned sideways. A second later, she slid forward, dropped, and righted herself in the water.

We had run up one side of a coral head and down the other. At that moment, I realized, the hull could be holed and the boat could be sinking, but the good news/bad news was that the *Gypsy Moon* was now afloat again and free to sink in deep water, where she would be beyond any hope of recovery. My imagination raced with the possible logistics and expense of what had just occurred.

To make matters worse, the sudden grounding had jerked the much smaller and lighter police boat to a stop. This caused the nylon towrope to go slack, allowing it to sink beneath the police boat's stern. The sinking line promptly fouled the propeller of one of the boat's twin outboard motors and parted.

In the darkness, I could hear the conversation of people aboard the police boat working to free the fouled prop, to no avail. That engine was out of service for the night. Eventually, what remained of the towrope was made fast again, and the towing operation continued under power from the remaining outboard engine. Now being propelled off center and towing the weight of a larger boat behind her, the police boat moved forward slowly in wide arcs, weaving from side to side like a drunken snake.

After running up on the coral head, I radioed the towboat to suggest to them that we had cut the corner of the reef and that we ought to look for deeper water going forward. The news that I could see our location and depth from a GPS unit and depth sounder on board cheered the crew of the police boat, which had neither device. From that point forward, they asked me to broadcast my depth on the radio at regular intervals, remaining especially alert to any depth below twelve feet. They used this information to choose a safe path to shore.

Though I find some black humor in the retelling of this tale, I hold my rescuers in no contempt. My mistakes that day preceded and greatly exceeded theirs, and I was fortunate and grateful to have their assistance. I was on a sailboat, for God's sake, and yet because of my needless rush to make port, I was calling for a tow like a child for his mama.

The police boat set me adrift where I could safely anchor in calm water, just outside Chalk Sound. Another tow would arrive the following morning to take me the rest of the way to Caicos Marina & Shipyard. Once at anchor, I checked the bilge and found it reassuringly dry. This meant that the boat had not been holed in the grounding on the reef, but there was still a possibility of serious structural damage. Early the following morning, I donned a swim mask and jumped into the preternaturally clear water to inspect the hull and rudder.

Recalling the painful sound I had heard the night before when the *Gypsy Moon* hit the reef, I was astonished to find not even a scrape in the paint from the bottom of the keel to the tip of the rudder. There was no damage at all. Herod's ghost had done his worst and had nothing to show for it. For this, thanks goes not only to my maker but to Endeavour Yacht Corporation, the maker of the *Gypsy Moon.*

Endeavour, formerly located in Largo, Florida, was once a mainstay of the boatbuilding industry in the United States. It has since gone the sad way of Pearson and other defunct boat builders, capsized by the ten percent "luxury tax" on boats that was enacted by Congress in the 1980s. Intended to soak "the rich," this tax instead dried up new-boat sales and decimated American manufacturers along with thousands of good jobs. Now the rich buy their boats from France, but the *Gypsy Moon* and hundreds of similar stout vessels made by Endeavour between 1974 and 1988 are still plying the seas in a testament to American craftsmanship.

Chapter 46

THE STRANGER

As happy as I was to arrive there with my boat in one piece, Providenciales itself was something of a disappointment. In fact, after having a look around I rather regretted that I had not kept going and taken advantage of several more days of fair weather to reach a more indigenous and diverse Caribbean culture in the Dominican Republic or even Puerto Rico.

Provo is the largest of the Turks and Caicos Islands, which geographically are part of the Bahamas. Like the Bahamas, they are marked by low elevation, poor, sandy soil, and low-growing vegetation. Politically, the Turks and Caicos are a territorial possession of Britain and under that nation's financial control. Locals blame the Brits for raising prices and making life generally more of a pain in the ass than it need be.

Owing perhaps to the fact that commercial development of the island first began only in the mid-1980s and has paused during economic downturns since then, what I found on Provo were nondescript expanses of land loosely connected by long, dry, dusty roads. Unlike Nassau, where it is possible to travel anywhere by bus, Provo has no system of cheap, dependable public transportation. Most people here either own or rent a car to get around, and those who cannot afford to pay the high island prices for gas walk or hitch a ride.

I was able to ride into town with a crew member of a dive boat at the marina when he left to buy spare parts. I planned to rent a car at the airport and scout out as many places as I could find that might be of interest to Susan whenever I returned to the island with her.

The traffic on Provo drives on the left side of the road. Although this was my first experience with left-handed driving, in no time I had the hang of it—or so I thought.

After renting a car at the airport and making sure I knew how to return there to catch a flight the next day, I found my way back to the marina. I got the *Gypsy Moon* tucked into her slip, signed papers for the harbormaster, and left for town again with pen and paper in hand. I was ready to learn everything there was to know about the island in the next six hours.

The roads on Provo are lonely, and the one that leads several miles off the main highway into Caicos Marina & Shipyard is lonelier than most. I had just begun driving obediently on the left side of this road when I came upon a trim, middle-aged man of Asian descent. He wore a collared shirt and long work pants that were covered in dust. He was on foot, but he was not hitchhiking. He was instead walking determinedly for the highway that was still a long way off. I slowed down to offer him a ride, and he got in.

This was the first time in thirty years that I had stopped along a road to offer a stranger a ride. I don't know why I stopped on this day. Perhaps I hoped to learn something of the local culture, but it was soon apparent that I would learn nothing from this man, as he spoke no English.

In silence we rode the remaining miles to the main highway. It was a long distance, and as we traveled it I thought about the time and effort I was saving the man who sat beside me. I imagined how grateful he must be for my kind gesture. I felt good about myself and about the good deed I had done.

When I stopped at the highway, I intended to turn left toward town. I was concentrating on driving on the left side of the road and focused intently on staying in the correct lane during the turn. What I was not concentrating on, and what I did not see, was the traffic speeding at me from the right. Thankfully my passenger was paying attention, as I otherwise would not be writing these words to you now.

As I began to turn left, the man seated next to me shouted, "Stop!" Startled, I abruptly obeyed. A second later, a line of speeding cars whizzed past my front bumper. I was so shaken by this near-death experience that I scarcely heard the man tell me, in perfect English, that his street would be coming up another mile after the turn.

Driving on the left side of the road is only part of what Americans planning to rent a car in Provo need to remember. Learning to look right before turning left is another. More important than even these skills, though, is the knowledge that when we give comfort to strangers, we are sometimes saved by the grace we receive in return—on the loneliest of roads, in the unlikeliest of places, and in the moment of our greatest need.

Chapter 47

THE GIFT

Standing in stark contrast to the rest of the island of Providenciales is an opulent greenway of high-end hotels, restaurants, and shops along the beachfront known as Grace Bay. Here I found wealthy vacationers and expats enjoying the high life beside the famously cerulean water. The fact that the nice grocery store on Grace Bay finds it necessary to pay for an armed guard to stand by the entrance and make eye contact with everyone who enters tells you all you need to know about the prevailing socioeconomic disparity.

There are ultrachic jewelry and clothing stores and luxury design studios clustered around the hotels and villas of Grace Bay, but if there were colorful colonies of artisans on Provo selling indigenous handicrafts and art, I never found them in the day I spent driving a rented car. Most of the local culture I did find seemed to have sprung up in service of the new tourism. Grace Bay had a born-yesterday kind of inauthenticity that reminded me of a movie lot in the California desert.

In every desert, however, there is an oasis. I found one on Provo at the Church of St. Monica, an Anglican church.

The Gift

I was on the island, after all, partly in service of a mission I had borrowed from the two-thousand-year-old story of the Magi, and I had in my possession a cargo of gifts meant to be given in honor of the Christ child. So I set out to find him. As the angels would have it, I found her instead.

A telephone call to the rectory of St. Monica's was answered by the rector's wife, who of course knew nothing of me or my voyage. She paved the way for my welcome nonetheless, and moments later a gentleman named Leon appeared at the marina. He extended official greetings on behalf of the pastor, who was visiting a sister parish on another island.

Leon came aboard and told me something of his former life working aboard cruise ships. He learned of my voyage, taking special interest in the *Gypsy Moon*'s self-steering wind vane, and he invited me to the Sunday service. There I would have the pleasure of hearing him accompany the choir on trumpet. He would also relate to the congregation the story of my seven-day solo voyage from Nassau, which I sensed they received as proof that God must indeed protect the fools of this world.

I arrived at St. Monica's early that Sunday morning, carrying under my arm the bundle of handmade treasures entrusted to me by the children in Raleigh. I took a seat halfway to the altar in the empty pews. All was quiet, and I was alone. At sea I had succumbed to the baser impulses of bachelor living, neglecting to shave or wash my face for two days. A clean shave that morning before church revealed the resulting eruption of scaly red skin across my nose and chin—a tendency inherited from my Irish ancestors. I looked like a man no more than two steps from a halfway house.

As I waited in the pew for redemption, I was struck by the contrast between the serenity of that setting and the chaos of the one at sea only two days before. It occurred to me that those separate worlds of peace and pandemonium envelop the same Earth and that we err to suppose when we are in the midst of one that we have somehow banished the other. The challenge is to find peace within the tumult. We achieve this not through wishful thinking that life on Earth will always be just, but by recalling the promise of Him who said, "In the world you have tribulation, but take courage; I have overcome the world."

A child—a girl of ten years—also arrived in the sanctuary early and, with a confidence unlike that of other young children, chose to sit directly behind the red-faced stranger and engage him in conversation. I learned of her life as the oldest of several children and her daily devotion to making lunches for, and looking after, her siblings. She told me of her father, who had died. Hearing of this sorrow, I straightened my posture and focused more keenly on her words, wondering if it was not perhaps out of some tender need that she had chosen to speak to me.

For my part, I told her of my journey and my gifts. I saw her eyes sparkle when I described the brilliant star that rose above the southern ocean on my last night at sea and that now seemed, however implausibly to a doubting world, to have guided me to this child, on this morning, in this place.

The other children would soon arrive, and they would be delighted to unwrap the many cards and small emblems of friendship I had brought. But before they did, I asked the little girl who had come to sit with me to accept the flag that had flown above the *Gypsy Moon* throughout the voyage, thoughtfully sewn by the children of my parish with the symbols of our faith: the cross, the cup, a fish, an angel, and a dove. She good-naturedly posed at the altar for a photograph, holding this flag. In her beaming smile at that moment, I found my way at last to the place where the Star of Bethlehem had come to rest.

Chapter 48

MAIDEN VOYAGE

Within a month's time the *Gypsy Moon*'s engine problems had been resolved. (I was told that a faulty fuel pump—not insufficient oil—had been the chief culprit.) It was February 2011. The boat was again ready for sea, and I was eager to head south. This time, Susan would be coming along for the planned offshore passage of three days to the Dominican Republic—her first.

I found the service at Caicos Marina & Shipyard friendly and the rates affordable, but this remote, undeveloped corner of the island suffers from an overabundance of sand fleas and no-see-ums after dark. That won't bother you at all if you're staying aboard an air-conditioned megayacht, but it made the one night Susan and I spent aboard our boat on Provo something less than a vacation. Her soft, smooth skin was a prime target for the little buggers, and she awoke the next morning looking as if she had been stricken with the chicken pox.

The highlight of our return trip to Provo was a chance meeting with some friendly Swiss sailors. They have spent half of each of the last twelve years wandering around the Caribbean and homeschooling their charming daughter, returning to work and live in Burgundy, France, for the other half. They invited us aboard their boat, the *Taua*, for wine and cheese the night before we were due to sail for the Dominican Republic. They planned to follow us there once they finished fitting out. It was good to share the camaraderie of people who didn't need us to explain why, exactly, we were bothering to cross an ocean in a sailboat.

The clear, shallow waters that extend sixty miles southeast of Providenciales mark the outer edge of a vast limestone shelf. Formed 135 million years ago in the Jurassic period, it supports the low-slung islands within the six-hundred-mile contiguous range of the Bahamas, including the Turks and Caicos. South of this rim, the sea runs much deeper and the islands rise markedly higher than any in the Bahamas, owing to eons of seismic activity in the Caribbean Plate.

Hispaniola is a large island 130 miles south of Providenciales. Its landmass is divided between the countries of Haiti to the west and the Dominican Republic to the east. The Haitian side has been deforested and its people impoverished from decades of subsistence farming, while the agricultural export and tourism economy of the Dominican Republic has preserved the people of that country and their land. With lush green mountains as tall as ten thousand feet, rich valleys, and cascading rivers, the Dominican Republic resembles the volcanic islands of the South Pacific.

After a night spent studying the chart and plotting a series of GPS waypoints and compass headings for a course generally south, we left Caicos shipyard early in the morning. With the ever-dependable easterly breeze, I had the sails up almost right away. The diesel engine was promptly retired, not to be summoned again for three days.

With a woman aboard, I became a tornado of helpful assistance in comparison to my usual despicable lethargy. I was able to keep Susan reasonably comfortable in the cockpit, where she had a reliable view of the horizon to maintain her equilibrium. Her seasickness waxed and waned. At its worst it dampened her appetite to a mild degree, and she did make one small offering to Neptune over the course of three days, but her spirit never faltered.

By noon of the second day at sea, Susan was stretched out in the cockpit in all her glory, basking naked in the sun and sipping a rum punch, her head propped against a pillow as she listened to the iPod play through the cockpit speakers. While 30-plus sunblock is an unavoidable rigor of genetics for me, Susan can achieve a California tan without much assistance, and in her case the overall effect is so much more appealing. Alas, she underestimated the strength of the Caribbean sun that day. By evening, she was pink and swaddled in a blanket beneath the dodger, where she remained as well buttoned as a parson's daughter for the remainder of the voyage.

It was such a thrill to see the outline of the Ile de la Tortue (Island of the Tortoise) come faintly into view off the coast of Haiti as we made our way south on the long first tack from Providenciales. It looks literally like a turtle on the sea—just as it did to the first explorers who named it. I felt a swell of pride in knowing that I was coming upon a place that is beyond the itinerary of any day trip from the United States. This, I thought, was a view of the horizon known only to voyagers, not fishing buddies on a weekend binge from Miami. I was crossing, at last, the long-awaited Rubicon of my boyhood dreams.

Chapter 49

THE PERFECT MAHIMAHI

Despite her mild seasickness and for reasons I didn't otherwise understand, Susan asked me repeatedly about fishing while we were underway for the Dominican Republic. She wanted to know when I would start fishing, how soon I would catch a fish, what I would do with the fish once I caught it, why I hadn't started fishing yet, and then again, when I would start fishing.

To be honest, as the one in charge of the bloody mess of cleaning and preparing the catch, I would much rather have opened a can of chickpeas and made a lovely meal of them sautéed in olive oil with red bell pepper, cumin, and sea salt, served over a wild rice medley and seasoned with parsley and cayenne. Everything in that dish comes from a can, a bag, or a jar that can be neatly stored in and retrieved from the ship's larder, not a writhing, indignant beast that must be ritually sacrificed before it is served.

Fishing aboard a sailboat underway involves trolling a line from a rod mounted on the stern rail. This method poses hazards to navigation regardless of whether one ever catches a fish. Twice while sailing offshore I have tacked or jibed without first thinking to reel in fifty yards of fishing line, only to discover that as the line passed under the boat during the turn, it became wrapped around the propeller. On both occasions I wound up playing Lloyd Bridges in an episode of *Sea Hunt*—jumping over the side in midocean with rigging knife at the ready to cut the line free. It is an eerie feeling to swim atop a mile of ocean, see nothing but a continuous gradient of blue descending beneath you into the abyss, and realize that you are one of the smallest living things in that world.

That feeling again came suddenly to mind as I heard an uncharacteristic whirring sound come from the drag on the fishing reel, about seventy-five miles off the coast of Hispaniola.

The open-faced reel and short, stubby rod that I keep aboard the *Gypsy Moon* are made for deep-sea fishing. I set the drag so that the amount of tension needed to strip line from the reel was just below the breaking point of the thirty-pound-test line. That means that a firm line will set the hook hard enough to keep smaller and medium-sized fish from getting away, while larger fish will strip line from the reel without breaking it unless they are—well, truly huge.

The only lure I bother to carry anymore is a ridiculous green lizard wearing a hula skirt. I don't understand why, but it is deadly seduction to mahimahi and just about everything else with teeth that swims. When a fish hits the lure, if he is not small enough to be towed along by the boat's motion under sail, the drag will clatter and clack as line is pulled backward off the reel. The noise made by the drag is usually a short series of halting staccatos, like the sound of a metronome with arrhythmia. On this occasion, however, line was flying off the reel as if it were a motorized spindle in a textile mill, and the noise it made was an even, electric hum.

Standing in disbelief at the stern rail as I watched the smoking reel, I didn't quite know what to do. Susan was apoplectic with excitement that we had finally caught something, but at this rate, I knew that all of the line would soon fly off the reel in the direction of West Africa along with whatever was pulling it.

About the time I could count the number of wraps of monofilament remaining on the metal spool, the great beast paused. When he did so, I gently eased the rod out of the holder and began to crank the handle of the reel, to no effect whatsoever.

So great was the weight on the line that the gear ratio of the reel could not overcome it. Undaunted, I positioned myself facing aft, with both feet braced against the cockpit coaming, and began what looked like ritual prayers to Mecca. Holding the butt of the rod in my abdomen, I leaned far backward, then far forward, and reeled up the slack in between like a madman. This tug-of-war went on for close to an hour, after which the fish was still clearly in no mood for surrender.

I would gain a few yards at a time, the fish would gain them back, and we remained at a draw. Susan was incredulous. Her past experience in snatching sunfish from farm ponds bore no resemblance to the blood feud taking place before her. Yet there was nothing to be done.

Eventually, I returned the rod to its holder on the stern rail and let the *Gypsy Moon* do battle for me. She fared no better. The rod stood there, thrumming and pumping from the strength of its quarry, and the line remained taut. After another ten minutes of this spectacle, I again tried the rod in my hands. Again the beast would give no quarter. I could not bring him a foot closer to the boat. It was as if I were trying to hoist an engine block up from the sea floor.

Unwilling to admit defeat, I had defeat handed to me when I pulled the rod back in one final, herculean effort and the line promptly snapped. Susan's disappointment at the lost fish was palpable but tempered by the realization that we probably didn't want to know just what sort of monster had gotten away. Had we managed to pull it alongside, we likely never could have brought it aboard, and if we had managed that, it remains unclear who would have become lunch for whom.

I did have some spare fishing line, and the dancing hula lizard, happily for all, had an understudy. My failed struggle with the great beast was proof at least that we were in prime fishing waters, and surely there would be other fish in the sea. Before long, the hula lizard would ride again to work his terrible temptation.

Not more than a half hour after fresh line was on the reel and back in the water, the drag began to sing a different song. This time the noise was more familiar. The halting *clack-clack-clack* signaled that the fish was large enough to activate the drag but too small to overwhelm it. Taking the rod in my hands, I felt a more manageable weight on the other end. Fifteen minutes later, a fat mahimahi, luminescent green and weighing about ten pounds, lay flopping in the cockpit.

When the fish had lost his color and his life and thus was ready to be prepared for the pan, Susan startled at the red blood coming from the path of my fillet knife. The richly vascularized, red meat of the common dolphinfish, or mahimahi, as it was only recently renamed to ease the conscience of American diners, has a texture closer to a fillet of beef than most other varieties of fish. I set about the task of preparing this one for dinner.

The two thick, fresh fillets that sat in the pan of the *Gypsy Moon*'s galley that afternoon off the coast of Hispaniola would have been a prize meal at any restaurant anywhere in the world. But before leaving on this passage, I had had neither the time nor the inclination to shop for the ingredients needed to make an elaborate presentation of what we might catch. The items I had on hand would have to do.

In the ship's larder I usually keep bags of ramen noodle soup. These make for a warm meal with enough fat and carbohydrates to be filling, and—importantly on a boat at sea—they can be prepared in one pot on a swing stove in all weathers. I began to eye one of these, in oriental flavor, next to jars of honey and olive oil that were visible in the cupboard. A plan evolved for a simple yet elegant preparation of the day's catch. What follows is the recipe for that meal, happily ever after known as Mike's Minute Mahi:

- Crush a package of oriental-flavored ramen noodles inside the closed bag using the heel of your palm until the noodles are evenly broken. Carefully open the bag and remove only the foil spice packet inside.
- Bring two cups of water to boil in a saucepan. Add the noodles without the spices and simmer for three minutes, or until tender. Drain and cover the noodles to keep warm.
- Add about ½ cup of olive oil to a skillet.
- Add about ¼ cup of honey to the olive oil, then add the spice packet and a pinch of sea salt. Stir these ingredients in the skillet over low heat until well blended.
- Add ½ cup of cashews to the skillet.
- Add the fillets to the skillet and coat thoroughly with the oil, honey, cashew, and spice and salt mixture. Cook the fillets over low heat until done and remove them to a bowl. Continue to reduce the sauce in the skillet over low heat for a minute or two until it is slightly thickened. Leaving a thin layer of sauce in the pan, reserve the remainder of the sauce in the bowl with the cooked fillets.
- Add the drained cooked noodles and parsley flakes to the remaining layer of sauce in the skillet and toss for a few seconds until the noodles are well coated.
- Divide the noodles between two plates and place a fillet on each bed of noodles; spoon the reserved sauce over the fillets.

- Lightly dust with grated Parmesan cheese, parsley, and cracked black pepper. Serve immediately.

Simply said, the meal prepared that afternoon, the last day at sea before our landfall in the Dominican Republic, was exemplary of an unforgettable time in our lives. Susan, already feeling queasy and made more so by the smell of fish blood mixed with salt water, was able to eat only a few bites, but what she did eat she savored. In hindsight, I can see that this fish and the meal it became are a metaphor of our life together.

What made the dish served that day off the coast of Hispaniola so memorable was the utter imperfection of its preparation and presentation. For starters, this was not the fish we had hoped for. That mythic, superlative specimen had fled to the bottom of the Atlantic with a disgruntled hula-lizard in its mouth. We were forced to accept instead a more moderate meal of the smaller fish that came our way. It would seem that for these obvious reasons, this could never be the perfect mahimahi, and yet it was.

Because the catch was sudden and unexpected, there was no time to plan an elaborate, nuanced presentation at the dinner table. The right opportunity could not wait for another day—there was no refrigeration on board. This was a moment made to be seized. The meal had to be prepared and served right then or not at all.

Because the fish had to be prepared in the rolling, pitching galley of a small boat and on the dim flame of an alcohol stove, the odds that it would be remarkable, in any event, were slim. Yet it was. Through what improvements we could impart using only our imagination and the few ingredients we had on hand, it became something sublime.

I had occasion months after this voyage to reflect upon that modest fish and its remarkable transformation in the galley of the *Gypsy*

Moon. I happened to be watching, of all things, a live Internet video stream of the royal wedding of Prince William and Kate Middleton, now the Duke and Duchess of Cambridge.

I had a strange feeling of paternalistic pride in seeing these two very young people express such hope in each other and in the institution of marriage in today's fractured society. I felt compelled to tell them so in a brief note of congratulations that I wrote on behalf of Susan and myself and mailed to London. Before I finished the letter I added the recipe for Mike's Minute Mahi with a postscript urging the newlyweds to give it a try. With characteristic British politeness, the royal couple's thanks were given to us in a very kind reply from the palace secretary, and that note is now a cherished keepsake of ours.

Of course, it is very unlikely that the duke and duchess will ever attempt my recipe, and their aides may wonder how anyone could suppose that ramen noodles are worthy of a royal recommendation. Nonetheless, it remains my hope that one day when the kitchen staff is busy and nothing else looks appealing, William and Kate will discover that mahimahi, like marriage itself, is what you make of it.

Unlike Kate's choice of William, I am no one's idea of Prince Charming, nor am I Susan's first husband. She threw that particular fish back into the sea long ago. Neither am I the one who got away—full of drama, excitement, and mystery, refusing to surrender and eventually snapping the line. I am instead the fish who chose to jump headlong into the boat. Our meeting was sudden and unexpected, and to make something worthwhile out of that moment we both had to seize it. We are so glad we did.

We are still in the kitchen, Susan and I. What we are making of our marriage from the dreams we have on hand, mixed with a dash of innocence and not an ounce of guile, is something sublime in all its imperfection. The resulting creation is greater than the sum of its parts. Now, at the twilight hour, just when it seemed I might wander forever alone on a bitter sea, I find that I am a woman's loving and faithful husband and the apple of her eye. Not a bad day's fishing, I'd say.

LATITUDE 19.82.84 N

LONGITUDE 70.73.11 W

COFRESI, DOMINICAN REPUBLIC

Chapter 50

THE VOYAGE TO COME

Susan and I landed safely at Cofresi, near Puerto Plata in the Dominican Republic, on February 24, 2011. On this island paradise, the voyage that began in Annapolis in August 2009 came to its happy conclusion, and with it, the story that this memoir was written to tell. So it seems, my friend, that you and I have reached at last our long-awaited harbor. I trust you have found something of value in the voyage and will take well-earned satisfaction in this rest from your labors.

As I write these words in early November 2011, the hurricane season is nearly over. With its passing, a new story will unfold for the *Gypsy Moon* and her crew. When that story will begin, where and how far it will lead, and what may be written of it, I cannot say. But wherever the stars may take us, a story very different from the one you have just read is sure to follow—not about a search for love, happiness, or the perfect mahimahi, as all of these treasures are now safely in your keeping. What waits for the *Gypsy Moon* over the horizon are waters yet uncharted and tales yet untold.

Plainly speaking, there are two choices immediately ahead: one is west, the other east. One takes the Windward Passage across a thousand miles of ocean to Panama and the canal, then forty days and forty-five hundred miles nonstop to the Marquesas. The other takes the Thorny Path through each of the well-loved islands of the Caribbean and goes no farther.

The first path leads around the world to latitudes of the heart so unfamiliar to a boy from Baltimore that he may never truly find his way back. The other follows a shorter and more familiar route, closer to home and safer from the dangers of wild imagination. Along either course, a man's only guiding light will be his heart, and from his heart alone will he find his heading.

I have learned enough on this voyage not to presume that I myself know, much less have the ability to tell others, what my heading will be. You and I will both know where the *Gypsy Moon* is bound when we see her wake, and no sooner. From whatever harbors may come, I hope to write of the wonders large and small as yet undiscovered there. Until that day, as every day, I ask for your prayers, and I give you mine.

Peace be with you, dear friend, and may you find in my words some sign of God's peace.

LATITUDE 19.55.33 N
LONGITUDE 75.8.54.60 W
GUANTÁNAMO BAY, CUBA

The Loss of the *Gypsy Moon*

In life there are dreams, and there are delusions. Wisdom lies in the ability to tell the difference between the two.

In the spring of 2009, when I resolved to begin the voyage that I boasted (but scarcely believed) would take me from Annapolis to Nassau, I sought the advice of a man technically proficient in the ways of diesel engines and the labyrinthine system of pumps, pulleys, gears, filters, and conduits necessary to make them go. This fellow was renowned throughout Chesapeake Bay as something of an oracle. He could be trusted, I was assured by more than a few sailors, to tell the truth about the repairs necessary to keep a boat off the bottom, and to work faithfully (albeit not cheaply) to complete them. For that reason, among others, I probably should have listened more closely to what he had to say.

Knowing where I was bound, this mechanic disregarded my initial request that he complete merely a routine, seasonal change of the *Gypsy Moon*'s oil and fuel filters and decided to look closer—close enough to see that her aging engine was in a worrisome state of disrepair. He scolded me that the boat wasn't safe to take out into the bay (where I had been sailing for the past year), much less on the ocean. Some of the repairs she needed most, in fact, were no longer even possible. I took his comments with the grain of salt reserved for advice given by those who stand to profit by it, but I also knew enough about the condition of the engine to recognize the ring of truth in what he said, even if I didn't care to hear it.

An inboard diesel engine is bolted at four corners onto reinforced fiberglass struts that form a rectangular mounting platform on the inside of the hull, near the stern. From the rear of the engine the propeller shaft emerges and exits the hull through a series of fittings designed to allow the shaft to turn freely while keeping the ocean from entering the boat. Because the propeller shaft must be angled and aligned to strictly measured tolerances in order to exit the hull cleanly, the engine must likewise be mounted at a proper height, angle, and alignment. Unlike a car engine, which spends its life in a more or less fixed, horizontal plane, the engine in a sailboat might be tossed up, down, and sideways by the motion of the boat and the condition of the surrounding seas. A boat that has spent its whole life serving lunch while chasing puffy white clouds on protected waters will subject its engine to little stress. The *Gypsy Moon* was not such a boat, nor had she led such a life, at least since I had acquired her in 2003.

The mechanic informed me that the position of the engine had shifted and that the propeller shaft was badly out of alignment, causing vibration that threatened eventually to rattle everything loose and sever the heavy shaft, which was already damaged and had to be replaced. To make matters worse, the large bolts and nuts of each of the rear motor mounts had rusted so badly over thirty years of exposure to salt water, salt air, and the humidity of southern waters that they were now an immovable lump of corroded metal. Any attempt to loosen and adjust them would break the mounts and cause irreparable structural damage to the engine block. The forward motor mount on the starboard side could be adjusted, I was told, but the mechanic offered to attempt that repair only if I understood that this might not succeed in aligning the propeller shaft, making all his work for naught.

I recognized in the mechanic's defeated tone as he explained the possible repairs, the same impassivity expressed by the doctors caring for my mother when they offered surgery to install a pacemaker in her heart just a few days before she died. Of course we went with the pacemaker, and of course this was never going to save her, and of course we, her well-meaning children, regretted suffering her the distraction and discomfort of that further ordeal during what turned out to be her last days on Earth. The mechanic, skilled though he was, hesitated to say what we were both thinking: that after thirty years, the necessary repairs were no longer worth the cost, and that the time had finally come to put the *Gypsy Moon* out to the gentler pastures of protected harbors, closer to home.

Of course I told him to attempt the repair, and of course he succeeded in completing it, because that is what watermen do. Men of this fellow's ilk have been keeping old boats together with wire and sealing wax for generations, along with the families who are fed by them. Before he finished he found many other, lesser flaws, some of which were added to the list of repairs and prolonged his work. More than five months passed before he was done. For his efforts I was presented with a ponderous bill that likely exceeded the market value of the entire vessel, but I would have paid even more to be spared the loss of what the *Gypsy Moon* embodied for me at that time in my life.

When I came to meet with this man on the Magothy River in August 2009, my boat was floating high and proud beside the dock.

What improvements and repairs he'd been able to perform were complete, and she was as ready as she would ever be for the journey that over the next two years and two thousand miles would become the story of this book. As he stood with me in the cockpit, I could see that in the end he, too, had been infected by the romance of what I planned to do. I could tell him nothing about the boat's engine or electronics that he did not already know, but when he tentatively asked about the operation of the wind vane, the characteristics of the boat under sail, and my intended ports of call, I could see the dream in his eyes. It is not wind or diesel or water but the engine of imagination that drives a man to begin a voyage, and that engine was running at full throttle. You could almost feel it in the air. It was not a matter of millimeters or angles or the metrics of mechanical propulsion anymore. What propelled the *Gypsy Moon* was a force far less powerful than what compelled her. She was compelled by a dream.

The dream was still alive when I landed at the airport in Puerto Plata, Dominican Republic, more than two years later, with plans to sail alone to Panama. It was January 6, 2012, almost a full year since the *Gypsy Moon* had arrived at Cofresi on a passage from the Turks and Caicos with my wife, Susan, as a slightly seasick but willing passenger. After signing a yearlong lease on a berth at Ocean World Marina, Susan and I had returned several times by air to visit the island while staying aboard the boat. We campaigned all across the country—from the ancient cobblestoned streets of the Zona Colonial in Santo Domingo, to the French bistros of Las Terrenas, to the hip seaside cabanas of Cabarete. We found these to be places of great beauty but also great sadness, where grinding poverty, limited opportunities for education, and petty official corruption consign so many people to the margins of society. Here in the Dominican Republic, as in so much of the Caribbean, the contented, smiling face presented to (mostly American) tourists at upscale resorts is largely a false one that conceals a darker and more desperate reality for the native population. Over the months when I visited the island, I began to feel an ugly sense of vanity in pursuing this rather expensive and pointless means of entertaining myself.

Were I a better man, or perhaps just a younger or more naïve one, I might have been compelled by these sympathies toward some heroic mission to improve the lot of native islanders, but I was not. On such matters I have become something of a cynic in my old age. I made a point of treating every man and woman I met with fairness and deference irrespective of his or her station in life, but beyond this I tried to check the uniquely American impulse to insist that everyone else in the world live as I do.

Over beers and *hamburguesas con queso* that night in Cofresi, in January 2012, I asked an American friend how he and his wife were enjoying living aboard their boat, which occupied the slip next to ours. It had been almost a year since they had arrived, having sold their house and most of what they owned. During that time they had provided invaluable help to Susan and me, while we were back in the States, by periodically running the *Gypsy Moon*'s engine and tending to her dock lines during a near-miss encounter with a hurricane. Now that I was about to cast off for Panama, a thousand miles away, it seemed the right time to ask some of the harder questions about just what it was we were all doing down there, so far from home.

The Dominican Republic is indeed a natural paradise, so it came as little surprise that my American friend and his wife had found happiness in their life aboard a boat in that foreign land. More surprising was my growing realization that this same contentment had somehow eluded me. The squalor and poverty I had passed on my way to the marina from the airport were still jarring. The opulence of the marina seemed only more garish and contrived by comparison. I was still very much a stranger in this place where my friends felt at home, even though I spoke the language and they did not. I feared that I had at last become an Ugly American, that loathsome creature incapable of long-term survival outside of tour buses, timeshares, and other escape pods of Western civilization.

For Susan, her passage of three days on the open sea to arrive in Cofresi had been a mildly unpleasant endurance contest, but living aboard the boat in a marina had proven to be little reward for the journey. The Spartan accommodations gave her a sore back and fitful sleep. Although she was a good sport and willing to endure these discomforts for my sake, I became less willing over time to ask her to do so. Yet still the dream of cruising the world that had first inspired the voyage persisted, and the thought of giving up that dream still represented a kind of psychic death that terrified me.

As I wrote in the preceding (and intended final) chapter of this book, I had two choices for the way ahead: one west, the other east. On that night in January 2012, drinking a beer with my American friend in Cofresi, I resolved to take the westward course.

My plan was suitably grandiose. I would leave the next morning and sail a thousand miles nonstop through the Windward Passage between Cuba and Haiti to arrive in Panama in ten days. I would leave the boat there, returning five months later to transit the canal and cross forty-three hundred miles of the Pacific in forty days to reach the Marquesas. As time permitted, I would continue around the world, covering as much water as I possibly could to finish the voyage as quickly as I could. If I were careful in my planning, I thought, I could complete a circumnavigation by sailing only a couple of months out of each year. At worst, I would plant my flag in some suitably remote part of the South Pacific and declare a fitting end to my quest.

Susan did not plan to accompany me on this voyage, nor did I wish for her to suffer that hardship. But she understood my need to go and vowed to wait patiently for my return from each leg. That was the plan.

I awoke to cloudy, drizzly skies in Cofresi but a continued beneficent forecast of eleven-knot winds and one-to-two-foot seas. The wind was expected to diminish to less than five knots between Haiti and Jamaica, with the seas becoming nearly calm. I worried about how much fuel I would have to use in that section of the passage just to keep moving. My worries were unfounded, though for reasons I scarcely could have imagined. On the morning of January 7, I set sail.

My first launch was a false start, as it had been on that rainy Thanksgiving Eve in Beaufort two years earlier. I unwittingly provoked a minor incident with the Dominican Navy and immigration department over the suspicious nature of my sudden, unannounced departure for Panama aboard an old sailboat moving at five knots, which apparently fits someone's profile of a dangerous drug runner. When I was an hour west of Cofresi, barefoot and reaching for the Windward Passage, I was suddenly overtaken by a motorboat manned by five armed guards screaming in Spanish about a form I had failed to fill out. One came aboard and escorted me back to my old slip in the marina, where for the next hour every compartment of my boat was subjected to a thorough ransacking under the guise of an "inspection." If I had been looking for a reason not to make the voyage that day, this would have been a good one. But after putting my vessel back in order and making encore farewells to my American friends, I paid the twenty-dollar departure tax I had foolishly overlooked and was permitted to leave.

The wind was not merely light but entirely absent that first morning and most of the afternoon. Both sails were limp, slapping haphazardly against the rigging as lumpy seas, rolling in from the northeast, gently rocked the boat from side to side. I rigged the wind vane with a large airfoil made to be lighter and more sensitive to gentle breezes, but there was not enough wind to hold a course. A frontal system that had been moving through the mountains of Hispaniola appeared to have stalled and was standing still. A misting rain fell. Nothing moved. I was loath to use the engine, knowing that even with a full tank and four spare cans of diesel lashed on deck, I had insufficient fuel to motor the entire distance to Panama. I needed to sail as much as I could, but I also needed to move. Looking at my watch and considering the schedule I had planned to follow to make eleven hundred miles in eleven days, I fired the engine and set the electronic autopilot for 314 degrees. The motor purred reassuringly as the *Gypsy Moon* settled into a six-knot pace on a following sea.

Several times that afternoon, when wavelets crested with foam would briefly appear, I stopped the engine and set the sails, only to lose speed and come to a standstill as the wind died. It was not until late in the day that the wind began to blow steadily from north of east. With this, the steering vane snapped to attention and went to work. I marveled once again at how effortlessly this device kept the boat on course, despite the unsteadying motion of following seas working against the rudder. I resolved someday soon to write a glowing letter to the manufacturer about the days, weeks, and hours of strenuous effort I had been spared by this astonishing contraption. I knew that when the time came for this device to mind the helm not for an hour or a day but for forty days and four thousand miles, across the Pacific, it would do so perfectly. But I also knew in that hour, perhaps for the first time in my life, that I never wanted that time to come.

Looking out on the open ocean that I have known for so many

days and nights and for which I have so often longed, I felt a new loneliness and a deeper longing than I have ever known at sea. I missed Susan as I always do on those rare occasions when we are apart, but it was more than that. Why had I not seen or felt this until I was two days into the voyage?

We all suffer the handicap of varying degrees of blindness and deafness to the most obvious and urgent realities that surround us, and if I have been more blind and deaf than most in the past, it has not been without consequence. But as I write these words in the stillness of a winter morning, looking out from the window of the tiny office Susan has made for me on the second floor of our home, I can see things a bit more clearly. The fog of thirty years has begun to lift, and what has been for so long a mystery to my own mind is drifting slowly into plain view.

Sailing has been a love of mine for almost as long as I can re-member, and that love endures. The lift and forward motion of a hull responding to the unseen force of wind upon canvas is pure magic and one of the essential delights of life. I highly recom-mend it. But over the years, the idea of sailing long distances over oceans, unobliged to return, became for me less about adventure than escape—a kind of trapdoor beneath the uncertain footing of a marriage and a personal and professional life that seemed at various times to teeter on the brink of collapse. Whatever the im-pending real or imagined "worst-case scenario," I believed I held the trump card as long as there was a boat waiting for me some-where with a clear escape route to the open ocean. But this kind of defense can be an obstacle to the growth that comes only when we allow ourselves to be fully exposed to, and accepting of, the vicissitudes of life. With no escape hatch, we have to face life head-on, admit our weakness, rely on our relationships, and trust others to catch us when we fall. In short, we have to join society and become fully immersed in it, for better or worse. This is a good thing. Man is a social animal.

Unwittingly, for me, the call of the open ocean began slowly to fade as this voyage and the people and experiences I encountered along the way dispelled my sense of despair and increased my sense of society. I had fallen in love, yes, but like a growing child for whom a teddy bear gradually becomes a less essential defense against the bogeyman, I had also become less fearful of the unknown and more willing to trust myself and those around me. Yet still, I had begun this last voyage, a man of sound mind, with plans to venture far away, alone, from everyone and everything I know and love. Why?

Truly, I do not know. Perhaps I needed to confront for myself, in the spiritual and physical darkness of an empty sea, the stark reality of what it would mean to leave a woman I truly, deeply, and passionately loved to pursue a quest that would separate us for months and thousands of miles. The voyage I had just begun would do that, I knew, and I had known that before I began. But I had not known until that moment, in my innermost heart, that this was no longer my dream, nor perhaps had it ever been. For the first time in my life, I was not afraid to say so. Somewhere in the ocean northwest of Haiti and northeast of Cuba, the bearings of a new plan and a change of course began to emerge.

I decided that the *Gypsy Moon* and I would have one last great sail together—not west or east as I had only recently intended, but north, six hundred miles to Miami. In the coming week I would bear safely off the coast of Cuba until I could turn north to reach the Florida Keys and Biscayne Bay. Once there I would find a marina that could arrange for the boat to be hauled and trucked to North Carolina, where the leaders of a summer camp who once imagined that they might have an oceangoing boat on which to train young sailors would see their dream fulfilled at last. Susan and I would find a small boat to scratch my sailing itch on day sails that would not unduly afflict her with the kind of sickness known to the open sea. This was my new plan, and my plan, once again, would be the occasion for much laughter among the angels.

On the morning of the second day at sea, after the moon had given way to blue skies and scattered clouds, I tried several times to reach Susan on the satellite phone and tell her of my change of heart. The satellite signal was uncharacteristically weak in this part of the ocean and had been for the past day. Only intermittently would the phone receive a signal strong enough to complete a call. Finally, at nine in the morning my call to Susan went through.

As our voices went in and out with the signal, there was little chance of a lengthy conversation, so I blurted out what I thought she most needed to hear. "I'm going to Miami instead of Panama," I shouted. She was tracking my position in real time over the Internet, through a GPS device on board, and I did not want her to worry that the boat was unmanned when it failed to turn south. Through her broken reply, I heard her ask why. "Because I miss you too much," I said, "and this is no longer fun for me. It's not my dream anymore. It's not what I want to do." Then the phone went dead.

The wind vane stood watches in the afternoon of the first day, all night, and all of the second day, until the *Gypsy Moon* was squarely in the teeth of the empty, trackless sea amidst Hispaniola, Cuba, and Great Inagua known as the Windward Passage. Throughout this time I lay awake in my bunk or slept in ninety-minute intervals, rising at night to scan the moonlit horizon for any sign of a ship. At one point on the first night, I spotted the lights of what might have been a cruise liner far to the north, but otherwise I saw not another vessel for two days.

After my phone call with Susan, the weather began to change.

In the dangerous game of escalating rationalizations that so often presages disaster, I looked for reasons not to be alarmed into action when the wind speed increased and exceeded the forecast. I told myself that the temporary effect of thermal inversion was the cause of the boisterous weather, as it had been last year around this time off the Berry Islands. I told myself that by sundown the wind and the motion of the boat would ease again. Had I not been so eager to justify this premise, it might have occurred to me that, unlike my position south of Grand Bahama and north of the Berry Islands the year before, there was nothing but open ocean to the north and no landmass for three thousand miles in that direction that could create a localized thermal inversion. The weather was changing, and for the worse. I just didn't want to believe it.

Further obscuring my sense of reason was the fact that I was on a heading off the wind, not slogging upwind against the waves. On a downwind point of sail a boat can carry much more canvas for much longer, as the wind rises, than would be comfortable sailing in the same weather upwind or on a beam reach. Even as the wind speed passed twenty knots, it made no sense to me, in my hobgoblin logic of the moment, to reef or change sails on my offwind heading. This seemed particularly true in view of my persistent assumption that the rise in wind speed and wave height that day would be brief. I thought it very likely that I would soon be lollygagging about the ocean in light winds again, making slow forward progress and casting longing glances in the direction of the boat's diesel engine.

By midafternoon, I had been neatly maneuvered by my own wishful thinking into a predicament. The wind was up, but the sea state seemed to have worsened disproportionately to the wind. The boat was now yawing uncomfortably with each passing wave, and the large light-air paddle on the wind vane was whipping about so wildly that it was nudging the vane off course. I found myself climbing into the cockpit every ten minutes to adjust the vane back to a proper heading and keep the boat from riding up into the wind. On one of these trips, I lost my footing in the cabin when a big wave passed under the keel. I was thrown hard to port as soon as I stood up, as though I had picked a fight with a man twice my size who had insisted that I sit right back down. The back of my head slammed hard against the teak cabin top—hard enough that I was more startled to be awake and seemingly unhurt than by the blow itself. I felt the back of my head for blood and found only a knot, then rested a moment to ensure that I wasn't going to black out. I made a mental note that I must be considerably more hardheaded than even my worst critics have imagined, and I thanked God for that.

As sloppy and unseamanlike as my sailing was, under these conditions, I was elated to see that the *Gypsy Moon* was keeping a steady seven-knot pace and regularly spiking eight to nine knots. We were hauling ass. At this rate, I thought I might make Miami in six days.

Yet as the slow rise of wind and seas continued unabated, it became clear that I should have reduced sail hours earlier. Before long, I decided that it would be imprudent, because of the unsteady motion of the boat, to go forward on deck at all unless it was absolutely necessary. Instead, from the security of the cockpit I slackened the mainsheet even further, to a lubberly and pitiful degree, in order to reduce the area of the mainsail exposed to the wind. This worked marvelously to steady the motion of the boat, but it also caused the jib—now obscured almost entirely by the main—to luff badly. I could hear the jib flapping like a tattered flag in a storm, but I was confident that it could take this abuse for a few hours until the wind slackened enough to allow a course change, when both sails would be needed once more. Again, my confidence was merely wishful thinking in disguise.

Two days and 191 miles into the voyage I had begun in Cofresi,

I was half-asleep in the pilot berth when I heard a loud and unusual noise on deck. Peering above the cabin top, I could see that the leeward jib sheet had gone slack. Investigating further, I saw that the running block for the jib sheet, which should have been upright and held fast by the taut line pulling like a rein on the sail, was dangling below the rub rail and banging against the hull. The jib had descended to a pitiful attitude at half-mast, like a worn-out sock falling down around a man's ankle. Going forward, I looked up to see that the jib halyard had parted at the top of the mast, allowing the jib to collapse to the foredeck and slacking the sheets. I was unable to retrieve the halyard and, as a result, would be unable to hoist a headsail until I reached a port for repairs. Without a jib, I could no longer sail effectively to a port or anyplace else that was not downwind of my position.

Whether it was laziness or wishful thinking that had kept me from going forward to reduce sail earlier in the day was now a moot point. My headsail had been reduced for me, and it was now my job to go and get it. I slipped on a safety harness, shackled myself to a jack line running fore and aft along the high side of the boat, and moved ahead in a crouch. The rise and fall of the boat had a familiar feel. Walking on deck in heavy weather was never as difficult to do as it was to imagine, and there were plenty of handholds along the way.

When I reached the bow, I planted my backside on the foredeck just aft of the anchor locker and braced my feet against the port and starboard bow chocks. The jib was still dangling halfway up the forestay and flailing badly. As I pulled it down hand over hand, most of the sail and the sheets washed over the leeward rail, creating a parachute effect that made it impossible to do anything but let the sail go. It remained connected to the boat only by two lines trailing in the water. The sail and lines swimming beside the boat, beneath the waves, seemed not unlike a man overboard, fouled in the wreckage of a ship's rigging, being pulled along and drowned. I recalled in that moment the king's ransom I had paid a well-known sailmaker, in Annapolis, to stitch that jib together by hand for me. I hired him to make that sail for twice the price I would have paid a faceless seamstress in the discount lofts of Kowloon, because I knew this jib would be my go-to sail for offshore conditions. I wanted a sail that was as bulletproof as it could be, and I wanted to look the man in the eye who would make it so. None of that seemed to matter now.

Watching this sail founder in the waves, I saw that the leech was battle-scarred and badly torn over two feet of its length from the flogging it had endured. The sail had survived no better than I in this test. I remembered the rigging knife in my pocket and considered for a moment simply cutting the sail and sheets loose to let all drift and sink in my wake, but something stopped me. That smacked of desperation and despair, and I wasn't ready to embrace either. The sail was repairable and still worth it, and so was my boat. From a seat in the cockpit, I bent loose the bowline knot that attached one of the sheets to the clew of the jib and began to haul the wet sail back into the boat, hand over hand, like the net of a Gloucester fisherman. It was a long and tedious process, followed by an equally long and tedious process of getting the tattered jib stowed in a sail bag, but eventually the rescue of the jib was completed. There would be no burials at sea that day. All the while, the *Gypsy Moon* continued to pull for Cuba under mainsail alone, slightly diminished in speed but still racing into danger.

Of the six hundred miles that separated me from Miami, four hundred passed through Old Bahama Channel—a navigational one-way street between the inhospitable shores of Cuba, to the south and west, and the impassable sand flats of the Bahama Banks, to the east and north. On the banks, ocean depths shoal rapidly in places from thousands of feet to just two or three, posing a risk of grounding to any boat that wanders there. With insufficient fuel to reach Miami under power and no effective means to beat upwind, if I kept my present heading I would soon pass a point of no return from which I would be unable to sail for any safe harbor outside of Cuba. For the time being, however, the gates of the Windward Passage were still open to me, south of my position. I was not yet in Cuban waters, and I could still head safely downwind in search of a repair port—if a repair port were to be found. That, it became clear, was very much a problem in this part of the world.

The only available port south of my position for the next three hundred miles was Port-au-Prince, a city that had become a crumbling, cholera-infested hovel of refugee camps, rape, and rampant violence in the wake of the earthquake that had devastated Haiti two years before. The chart books, all of which were written before the earthquake, advised strongly against any landfall in Haiti because of crime and poor facilities. Port-au-Prince was also well off the heading of my newly revised intended destination. I imagined the malevolence that likely awaited me anywhere in Haiti as the captain of a well-stocked, hobbled sailboat in need of new rigging for a pleasure cruise back to the United States. I needed a better option.

The island of Great Inagua was well within my fuel range, to the north, but the chart books warned that it was encircled by dangerous reefs. It offered only an open roadstead for an anchorage that was untenable in anything but a due-east wind. There was no marina or repair facility—only a government dock affected by a strong tidal surge, where boats were not welcome to linger. Motoring there could take days, against the northeasterly winds and swells. A landfall in the Turks and Caicos was out of the question, for the same reason.

With a growing sense of defeat, I resolved to turn east and give back all the hard-won miles I had traveled in two days since leaving Cofresi. By going back, I thought, I would at least find a safe, navigable harbor and a place to gather my thoughts for the next step. As I jibed the boat to find my new heading, it was a sign of growing mental fatigue that I made no effort to ease the sheet as the boom, whipped like a reed by the rising wind, swung smartly across the deck and crashed to a stop.

Headed east for the first time in two days, the *Gypsy Moon* reared up and bucked unwillingly against the trade winds and seas slamming into her bow. With the engine at full throttle, I could barely make any way. No sooner had I resolved to return to where I had started than it was clear that like it or not, I was going someplace I had never imagined.

I looked again to Haiti. Cap Haitien on the northern coast was more renowned among sailors, but it was too far east, separated from my position by seventy-five miles of contrary wind and waves. I was much farther from Port-au-Prince—a hundred and seventy-five miles away—but it was due south of my position and a straight downwind shot, with the waves behind me. Cholera and crime be damned, that was the place where I knew I must go. In fewer than twelve hours, if all went well, I would be in the lee of Haiti's northwestern point, where I could expect the wind and the seas to diminish considerably for the remaining hundred miles or so of the journey to Port-au-Prince. Perhaps there was a poor fisherman there, I thought, for whose family the *Gypsy Moon* would make a better gift than the well-loved children of a summer camp on the North Carolina coast.

It was by then getting late in the day. I was very tired, fairly banged up, and having difficulty keeping the boat on an even keel through the troughs of large waves approaching just aft of her port beam. The port and starboard steering control lines for the wind vane had some-how slipped off the steering wheel and become a disorderly mess during the various tacks and jibes of the past hour. The port control line was supposed to wrap counterclockwise around the wheel guide (or was it clockwise?) and the starboard line in the opposite direction, leading through two pulleys stacked on the port cockpit coaming, then aft to the vane rudder on the transom. As I attempted again and again the seemingly simple task of reorganizing the steering control lines and resetting the vane, I was having no success in restoring the proper operation of the self-steering gear. Unable to discern my er-ror, I sensed my resolve weakening as the first tinges of seasickness in twenty years of offshore sailing began to wash over me. This is how it must happen, I thought, when otherwise competent people, under the stress of deteriorating conditions and physical and mental fatigue, lose the ability to solve simple problems and start compound-ing their mistakes. I began to feel strangely frail and unsure of myself. One hears such stories, told of experienced mountain climbers who become disoriented and freeze to death, their bodies later discovered lying mere yards from safety. If this were the valley of the shadow of death, I thought, surely goodness and mercy were not following in my wake at the moment.

Blast the damned self-steering, I finally decided. I had more than enough fuel to reach Port-au-Prince under power, and although I could make better time sailing in this wind, running the engine would keep the batteries topped up, the electronic autopilot whirring, and the running lights burning brightly as I moved slowly closer to shore amid hazardous shipping traffic during the night. I snapped on my harness and tether, grabbed a rat's nest of sail ties in one hand, and made my way forward to lower the main. This would be a real rodeo, and I knew it.

The mainsail dropped to the deck obediently enough, but flaking it down onto the boom and getting it secured in those conditions was like a calf-roping contest involving a very large and unhappy calf. My task was to use one arm to gather and tie down 207 square feet of flying mainsail into neat accordion folds on top of the boom while using the other to keep a choke hold on the boom as the boat rocked from side to side and rose and fell between six and ten feet with each passing wave. My conquest of the mainsail in these conditions restored my confidence, and I moved back to the cockpit with renewed resolve. I was ill and tired, but I had at last found a sustainable heading and a plan that appeared likely to succeed in getting me and my boat to safety. Then, in an instant, everything changed again.

I don't remember seeing the wave. It is difficult to estimate the size of these things, but the larger ones I had seen so far that afternoon rose well above my head as I stood upon a deck that was already three feet above the waterline. Most were ten feet high, I would say—hardly the stuff of sailing lore but plenty big enough to make life awkward aboard a thirty-two-foot boat, and a far sight larger than what the weatherman had promised. The smaller waves were six feet or so. No matter what the weather, though, every once in a while anomalous waves do come along. I'm not talking about apocalyptic events or legends of Hollywood fame. Some waves just happen to be a good bit larger than the mean, as any kid floating expectantly on a surfboard at the beach will tell you. I would recognize the passing of such waves on long watches at night. For hours on end the boat would keep a familiar rhythm of movement until, suddenly, one particular swell would lift dishes and cups out of their racks and send them hurtling like missiles to leeward. The wave would roll past just as quickly as it had come, and I would return the scattered tableware to its hidey-hole, where it would rest again undisturbed for hours or days thereafter.

This wave was different, though how much so I cannot say, because it hit me from behind. I dare not guess its size. Given any license whatsoever, the Irishman in me would embroider it with an undeserved order of magnitude and malevolence. I can tell you only that I was facing forward, in the companionway, when I felt the weight of my 11,700-pound vessel being lifted upward and turned sideways, the way a child might lift a bath toy. This was followed by a brief interval during which the entire boat seemed to drop through the air, as if she had been rolled off a tall building. Then came a loud crash as the boat landed hard on her beam end in the trough of the wave, followed abruptly by an unnatural silence.

Diesel engines are hard to kill. I know this from years of murderous effort. I have run them to within an inch of their lives on empty crankcases, clogged seawater intakes, dirty fuel filters, and fluky alternators. In the face of these depredations the diesel engine will succumb—never suddenly but slowly—by throttling gradually downward to a begrudging, lingering end, like an aging prizefighter. On this day in the ocean somewhere between Cuba and Haiti, in a knockdown from an unseen wave, the engine of the *Gypsy Moon* was stopped like a man bludgeoned with a sledgehammer. There was not a cough or a rumble or a sputter. There was only a crash from the engine compartment, followed by the cessation of all noise and movement. I knew in that instant that the damage was grave and the prognosis grim.

The *Gypsy Moon*'s engine had not "run out" of anything. It had plenty of fuel and oil and water. The considerable force of its revolving motion had been stopped, physically and abruptly, by an immovable object. I was in no condition to empty the cockpit lazarette and lower myself to the bilge for a close inspection of the tight spaces under the engine, but it didn't matter. I knew that what *had* happened was exactly what a trusted mechanic on the Magothy River had told me *could* happen.

Human nature being what it is, hope springs eternal in such moments. And so I climbed into the cockpit and pressed the ignition switch to express the polite request that the engine simply dust itself off and get back to work. The starter responded with a thin electric buzz and nothing more, as I had known it surely would. I was dead in the water, with no headsail and no engine, with no ability to sail anywhere but downwind, and with no serviceable repair port within three hundred miles downwind of my position.

No longer underway, the boat began rolling badly in the swells, and I became violently, impressively ill. Succeeding involuntary spasms of projectile vomiting into the galley sink momentarily relieved the nausea, but these were followed by painful dry heaves. The unmistakable return of the pineapple juice I had drunk eight hours earlier was a complete surprise.

It was at best a guess, but I surmised that the force of the engine falling sideways in the knockdown had sheared off or shifted the rear motor mounts. An engine runs by manner of revolution, and the only thing that could have stopped the motor so abruptly had to do so by stopping it from turning. This meant that the propeller shaft had been jammed sideways against the hull in the knockdown, and for that to occur the engine must have moved. A moving engine meant a broken engine, and a broken engine, at this age and place in the life of the *Gypsy Moon*, meant a worthless engine. From years of yacht ownership I have acquired an intuition that tells me when something has occurred that is going to cost an obscene amount of money. This was one of those times. My royal carriage had very abruptly become a pumpkin shard, and the wise warning of the mechanic floated to me over the ocean like the unheeded advice of a fairy godmother. The *Gypsy Moon* was now a drifting wreck, and I was a man in need of help.

I have carried an Emergency Position Indicating Radio Beacon aboard the several oceangoing boats I have owned since 1987. In twenty-four years, I had never turned one on. I did that day.

If my confidence was warranted, the EPIRB would send a signal identifying my vessel and giving the coordinates of my position to a satellite monitored by a search and rescue center somewhere on the Eastern Seaboard, where the coast guard would with all deliberate speed determine whether my signal, among the dozens of false alarms and prank signals they receive every day, was genuine. The brilliant strobe light of the EPIRB confirmed its operation, and in the darkness of the cabin it appeared for a moment that an ambulance had arrived on the scene. Climbing the companionway steps only part of the way in order to lean into the cockpit, I used the enormous bag containing my torn jib to wedge the device in place, upright, where the antenna could transmit a clear signal into the night sky.

For a few minutes, I simply waited in the darkness for help. When I had last checked my position, I had been more than seventy miles from land and thus well out of VHF radio range. I also hadn't seen another ship for two days, so I hardly thought there was much point in a radio call. All the same, in a nod to proper seamanlike procedure, I decided to make a Pan Pan call just to be sure. "Pan Pan" is the radio code one step below "Mayday" in degree of urgency and is used to request assistance in moments of dangerous but non-life-threatening distress.

"Pan Pan, Pan Pan, Pan Pan. This is the sailing vessel *Gypsy Moon*," I began my broadcast. I told the unseen listener, believing all the while that I was talking only to myself, about the loss of my jib halyard, the knockdown that had damaged my engine, and my resulting inability to make way in any direction but downwind. Only Jamaica and South America lay in my direct path, some three hundred and six hundred miles away, respectively.

To my surprise—no, my astonishment—the captain of a British-flagged freighter, the *Paramount Helsinki*, answered my call and, in a thick Eastern European accent, stated that he had already begun heading for my position. He was eight miles away. Sticking my head out into the cockpit, I surveyed the night horizon and saw nothing—not even a light. When he asked what assistance I needed, I said I wanted a tow to a repair port. There was a long silence. The captain came back on the radio to say, with an almost quaint politeness that I scarcely deserved, that he was a *"beeg* freighter" and could not effect a tow. He could rescue me, not my boat.

About this time, a young American voice from a vessel identifying itself only as US Warship 913 hailed me and asked for the coordinates of my position. He, too, could offer only a rescue, not a tow to a repair port. After some initial particulars, he pointedly asked whether I would agree to abandon ship. His question dumbfounded me. I had never heard of abandoning a ship unless it was sinking or on fire. But the officer's request helped me to understand the hard reality of my situation.

I was six hundred miles from American waters, floating in the ocean on a mortally wounded boat between two Third World countries, neither of which presented any realistic options for dockage or repairs. This was not a Florida towboat operator calling me on a Sunday afternoon to arrange for a trip back to a marina in Biscayne Bay. This was big-boy trouble I had gotten myself into. I made sure the radio was off while I vomited ferociously again.

It was time to take stock of my position. My thirty-year-old boat (thirty-three, to be exact), which leaked like a sieve from every port light and deck fitting and on a good day in a better economy might be worth $10,000, was likely damaged beyond her value. Even if she could be repaired, there was no competent repair facility within three hundred miles of my position. The boat was not only uninsured but uninsurable, due to her age and condition and the remote waters in which she was sailing. I was in no mood and no shape to float three hundred miles to Jamaica, where I planned to do God-knew-what, on a boat with (soon-to-be) dead batteries, no lights, no motor, and only one working sail. When I considered the additional cost of storing, repairing, and retrieving the boat intact from her current predicament, not to mention how smoothly a Jamaican engine replacement project would likely go, the dollar signs whirred in my imagination like a financial horror movie.

Both ships in the area were monitoring my radio broadcasts. I called them back to advise that I would agree to "give up the ship." Those words have special nautical significance going back to Captain James Lawrence, who first uttered them aboard the US frigate *Chesapeake* in 1813, preceded by the word "don't." History tells us that even Captain Lawrence had to give up his ship, and, alas, so did I, though I would be a liar if I suggested that I did so unwillingly at the time.

The *Paramount Helsinki* was headed to the island of St. Lucia, in the far eastern Caribbean, and would not make port for another two days. US Warship 913 planned to make port by the next day at the naval base in Guantánamo Bay, Cuba, where I could board a flight to Miami. I opted to go with the Yanks.

The *Paramount Helsinki* continued to steam toward my position and arrived there first, even though it would not be called upon to perform the rescue. Demonstrating the courtesy, charity, and brotherly concern that are the rule among seamen everywhere on the open ocean, the *Helsinki* stood by my position until the rescue detail reported that it was in the vicinity, and only then did it slowly move on. I expressed my sincere thanks to the captain as I watched the big freighter steam away into the night, imagining the wonderful experience I might have had among his crew during the two-day voyage to St. Lucia.

The officer on US Warship 913 gently warned me not to be alarmed when the rescue detail suddenly appeared out of nowhere in a black boat, wearing the blacked-out gear they used for the element of surprise during hostile nighttime operations. When the rescue team finally arrived, formally dressed for the occasion, the seas were way up. While still several yards away, the coxswain shouted a question to me with surprising gravity: "Sir, are you prepared to give up the ship?"

There was that question again. I hesitated—why, I don't know—before saying yes, albeit with a measure of sadness and regret that had not fully registered with me until that moment. Surely there were dozens of things I could have done and should have done to avoid that ultimatum. One careless mistake had compounded another to bring me to this place. "My kingdom for a jib halyard," I thought. Perhaps if it had remained my plan, as it had been for so long, to take the *Gypsy Moon* around the world and far away from everything that I now held dear, I would have been the man to do the things and avoid the mistakes that had brought me to this current pitiable circumstance. But all that was done, then. It was time to go.

Earlier, my rescuers had informed me that they planned to rig the *Gypsy Moon* with multiple strobe lights and radar reflectors and to spray-paint both sides of the hull with USCG OK in giant orange letters, to ward off false reports of distress by other boats. However, in view of the sea state when the rescue detail arrived, these plans were scrubbed. I was handed only a small orange life jacket with a nine-hour strobe light to hang on the stern rail. Then it was time to board the rescue boat, which proved to be no easy task.

I found myself perched on the port rub rail, hanging on to the lifelines and the wildly swinging boom, trying to time the sequence of the waves that were raising both boats like opposite ends of a seesaw. The *Gypsy Moon* was still rolling badly.

I have great admiration for the three young men and one young woman on the small-boat rescue detail who kept at it until they finally pulled me aboard with what little luggage I could salvage. I learned that US Warship 913 is actually the US Coast Guard cutter *Mohawk*. The name is painted plainly on the hull but is concealed in radio broadcasts for security purposes. I was brought alongside, and the rescue boat with all of us aboard was hoisted up the side, again with great difficulty because of the rolling of the 278-foot cutter in the rough seas. The *Gypsy Moon* was set adrift through the Windward Passage, where she will someday hit South America if she isn't destroyed for target practice by the coast guard beforehand. When I looked back at her from the rescue boat for the last time to say good-bye that night, I was struck by the fine figure she cut upon the open ocean, surprisingly beautiful and floating high and proud, as she will always be in my memory.

Once aboard the *Mohawk*, I was greeted by the captain and taken straight to the corpsman for an examination. He located the lump on the back of my head, but he seemed satisfied that I had never lost consciousness and felt entirely fine. I was given a meal made to order by the mess crew, a steady stream of conversation with some of the finest young people you would ever want to meet, Cadillac quarters to share with a senior chief petty officer, and a hot shower. My ensuing daylong cruise to Guantánamo, during which I spent most of my time on the bridge chatting up the junior officers and staff, was a seminar on the wonderful job the men and women of the coast guard are doing to protect the people of the United States. I hereby take back my disparaging remarks about the coast guard, recorded earlier in this book, about the dismasting of my brother's sailboat in 1976. If anything, this latest incident demonstrates nothing so well as the fact that I have been a burden and a nuisance to the coast guard my entire life. Be that as it may, I felt a surge of patriotism and pride in seeing these young people in action, and my hat goes off to them.

The next day, one of the crew of the *Mohawk* told me that when looking down from the bridge at the rescue operation, he'd been able to see the keel of my boat come out of the water as each wave rolled her onto her side. He estimated that the seas were running eight to ten feet at regular intervals, with some higher swells. "I've got to give you some props," he said, "for being so calm on the radio. Had it been me out there on that boat all alone with no engine in this weather, I would have been freaking out."

The compliment was undeserved. The truth be told, I was never in any real danger on the *Gypsy Moon* that night or in all the years I sailed aboard her. In our last hours together, in the Windward Passage, she took a sucker punch in the back from a rogue wave and came up fighting. She defended me to the end, and in the end, I was the one who walked away from the fight. It was bittersweet solace to hear the young man's words.

So there you have it. I'm a landlubber now, looking for a bridge club and a gardening group to join. (If you have read this far in the book, you will recognize that last remark for the heinous lie that it is. At this very hour, I am carrying on a robust correspondence with a shipyard in Wareham, Massachusetts, concerning the construction of a twelve-foot gaff-rigged wooden catboat that I intend to name *Honor Bright*. She will not cross oceans, but she will have a tale to tell, mark my words.)

The *Gypsy Moon* may still be on the ocean somewhere today, and could yet cruise the world. With Godspeed, perhaps she'll even round Cape Horn of her own accord. I wouldn't put it past her, but

I must now put that past myself. For a man to know his own heart is a great gift, and though it took me two thousand miles and two years to come to this knowledge, I now realize that my treasure is closer to home, with a woman I love and not on a lonely ocean by myself, pursuing a delusion that I once mistook for a dream.

I do not have the first regret to have made the voyage, the loss of the *Gypsy Moon* notwithstanding. Had I not decided to sail from Annapolis on what I and everyone else at the time thought would surely be a boondoggle, and were it not for God's silence and my intuition, that night on the porch in Beaufort, that I should set sail for Nassau, I would be poorer in spirit, less wise, and less well loved than I am today. I had a great ride on a great boat, and without her I never would have met the love of my life. I wouldn't have it any other way.

© 2013 Jeffrey L. Ward